SMILE!

How to Elevate Your Dental Practice

By Empowering Your Office Team

Gary Lim, M.A.

with

Dr. Bruce Stewart, DDS

DORATO PRESS

Dedicated to my wife Judy and our daughter Michelle,

both of whom continue to keep me looking ahead

to what might be, what can be, and what will be.

FIRST EDITION

Publisher's Cataloging-in-Publication Data

Names: Lim, Gary, author. | Stewart, Bruce, collaborator.

Title: SMILE! How to elevate your dental practice by empowering your office team/ by Gary Lim with Bruce Stewart

Description: Dorato Press trade paperback edition. | New York : Dorato Press, 2017.

Identifiers: ISBN 978-0692839553 (softcover)

Subjects: LCSH: Business. | Dental offices. | Customer service.

For further information:
315-885-1532
www.SmileToElevate.com
www.AurariusLLC.com

Introduction

The dental industry, not unlike many other service industries, continues to face waves of transition. Insurance changes, competition from regional managed-care dental companies, the economy, and consumer finances have changed the way patients have looked at their dental care, and how dentists consider patients.

As revenue has fluctuated for some dental practices, many owner-dentists look carefully at their business expenses, from marketing and advertising to staffing. Unfortunately, many owner-dentists also tend to look upon their office staff primarily as contributors to expense.

This is a natural tendency, and could apply to more than just the non-clinical office staff (i.e. those who are not dental assistants or hygienists). In the worst case, some practice owners look at clerical or administrative staff as truly "overhead", and dental assistants and hygienists as a required expense.

After all, the dentist's activities bring revenue to the business. And many business owners in general think that the main objective is to maximize revenue while minimizing expense.

While this thinking is technically true, I'd like you to consider this novel thought:

The dental office team (clinical and non-clinical) is actually a resource which, when properly utilized, can **generate revenue** instead of merely being a cost center!

How might that be, you ask? After all, if the dentist is the one generating the revenue, everyone else must be subtracting from revenue in the form of an expense, right?

It's all in your perspective. If you view your office team as participating in revenue generation, you will choose to do some things differently with that perspective in mind.

If you view your office team as merely an expenditure, in tougher times all you'll think about is how to cut expenses, including your team members.

Amidst this parable of two dentists who happen to meet at an annual American Dental Association conference in San Francisco, I lay out for you the framework from which you should consider your office staff, your office "team" instead. This is an approach that I know can work, as I have seen the results within the practice of my collaborator on this work, owner-dentist Bruce Stewart D.D.S.

Dr. Stewart has used many of the concepts and tactics you'll shortly be reading more about, to build his business and the strength of his patient/client base. From a combination of Bruce's decades of practice ownership, along with my knowledge of the keys to successful businesses from many years of consulting work, I've been able to structure this framework for your success, embodied in the acronym SMILE.

I appreciate all the time Bruce spent talking with me at my request. Without those long conversations, I wouldn't have been able to craft SMILE and have it fit the way it does. By the way, as you'll soon read, the distinction I make between the terms "patient" and "client" is deliberate.

So come along on the journey with us, open your minds, and SMILE to elevate your dental practice!

Gary Lim
Gary@SmileToElevate.com
http://www.SmileToElevate.com

P.S. Though the main characters and their stories are fictional, I use actual restaurants in San Francisco as literary settings. No guarantees that you'll be able to get a table as easily as our main characters did!

Contents

"Your work is going to fill a large part of your life, and the only way to be truly satisfied is to do what you believe is great work. And the only way to do great work is to love what you do."

— Steve Jobs

"The difference between a successful person and others is not a lack of strength, not a lack of knowledge, but rather a lack of will."

— Vince Lombardi

Prologue – The Dentist

It was a beautiful day, a fact completely lost on the morning walker, as he looked out blankly over the classic postcard scenery. The brilliant morning sun lit up the facades of Alcatraz, creating an almost glowing haze against the backdrop of the surrounding water. The island seemed almost inviting as it defied its dark past. Light glinted off the gentle waves lapping in the San Francisco Bay, and reflected off the walls of the brooding, silent structure.

The man out for a walk stood glumly on the sloping sidewalk. His dark windbreaker worn over his sweater and khakis outlined a posture that suggested defeat. A full head of brown, slightly-graying hair rustled gently in the wind. His tall, trim frame reminded one of an active athlete, perhaps a runner or a tennis player, in younger days. The morning walker lifted his chin, turned his eyes skyward, and inhaled deeply.

Dr. Joel Chenoski filled his lungs with the crisp clear air, as a shiver ran through his body. Had he not been so wrapped up in his own misery, his nose would have noted the sharp contrast of coffee aromas and wharf-side marine odors.

From where he stood, partly up the hill on Larkin Street, he could see other early morning walkers out for some fresh air before breakfast. In the not-so-distant past, the quietness, the cool air, and the scenery had always invigorated him and rousted his appetite for a good breakfast.

But this morning Joel was neither invigorated nor hungry. He hadn't slept very well the night before. Then again, he never slept well the first night in a hotel.

First night or not, he thought dejectedly, he probably wouldn't have slept anyway. Too many thoughts bounced off the walls of his mind, some going in circles. Thoughts and worries that continued to dance and refused to settle.

These days, he worried about his dental practice often. Even though everything he'd read proclaimed the economy to be gathering steam, Joel didn't see it in his bottom line.

Or on his top line either. His revenues had either stayed level or declined over the past several years, and more and more, he worried about how much longer he could manage to keep his office afloat.

Expenses at the office increased steadily, because he had to recognize that people expected raises. But even though salaries continued to grow, his revenues did not. And lately, his office staff didn't seem to show the type of effort that he hoped they would.

During busy times, there didn't appear to be any problems. But when the office quieted down and empty appointment slots appeared on the calendar, the members of his office staff started to get on each other's nerves. Their bickering touched upon some of the most incredibly minor things he could even imagine.

Joel started to walk down the hill along the left side of Larkin, and turned into Ghirardelli Square. A few steps later, he reached the circular fountain in the middle of the square. He sat down on the edge of it, as the cool feeling of the concrete leaked through the thin fabric of his khakis.

Yep, he thought glumly, what a mess. Some of his office staff would act like bullies, and some would be loners and try to avoid contact with others. He needed them to work together and communicate with each other, but they refused, at least by their actions, anyway. During busy times, he simply had no time to micromanage that.

Why couldn't they take the initiative to do what's right, he thought with irritation, as he slapped himself on the right thigh. A passer-by heard the sound, saw Joel's display of silent emotion, gave him a quick look up-and-down, and veered away from the fountain.

And then there's the office manager, Joel mused, as the train of his thoughts continued to gather speed. She goes off in her own direction and doesn't bother to tell him or anyone else.

Sometime later, when he asks her what the status is on a specific project or task, she gives him a short, curt answer as if it's none of his business. This last recollection put Joel on a slow burn.

It's his practice, his business, and he pays all the bills. Yet his office manager gives him attitude, and he can't bring himself to hold her accountable for things she lets fall through the cracks.

But he really didn't know why, and that angered him.

The air was cool, crisp, with a chilly edge, typical of an early fall morning in the City by the Bay, but Joel was completely unaffected by the brisk envelope. Brow glistening with perspiration, he continued lost in his thoughts.

Over lunch breaks at the office, he would occasionally hear some of his long-time staff members say that it didn't seem to be much fun to come to the office anymore. And he even overheard one of them remark to another:

"You know, it's not even much fun to be around Dr. Chenoski anymore. It's like he's different than before. This place is just a job."

I'm no longer fun to be around?! Joel fumed at the thought. She should talk! As for being just a job, how about being better at it, doing more, instead of just costing me money!

His now runaway train of thoughts careened at full speed, as Joel pounded his fist on the edge of the stone fountain. Immediately he regretted it. Another morning walker eyed Joel out of the corner of his eye, and changed course in mid-stride to give him a wider berth.

As he shook out his stinging right hand, Joel thought, well there's some truth to that. He no longer enjoyed going to work like he used to.

He thought back to the early days, when he first started out. He remembered that in the beginning, even during the slow times, he still had a sense of excitement and hope about what could be.

His wife Lora worked at the front desk, though on some days having someone at the front desk didn't really matter. During empty appointment slots, he and Lora would allow themselves an episode of *Perry Mason* or some other rerun, on the old TV in the back office.

Even though they often felt uncertainty and worry, they both still had a sense of anticipation of how they could build the practice.

Joel stood up from his seat on the fountain and strode over to one of the coffee shops. Lora had stayed at home, because they didn't think they could afford for her to attend the American Dental Association annual meeting in San Francisco this year.

Maybe even he shouldn't be attending, but he figured, this is probably the last time. Heck, by this time next year he might be working for Vail Dental instead of still having his practice.

With a sigh, he stepped up to the coffee stand in the square.

"A decaf with cream and sweetener please."

Joel paid for the coffee and started back in the direction of his hotel near Fisherman's Wharf. The meeting sessions would start soon, and he had to catch the shuttle bus from his hotel to the conference location.

To avoid the extra cost of staying at the conference hotel downtown, Joel had booked a room at the Courtyard by the Wharf using airline miles that he had left in his account. That saved him the hotel expense.

As he walked back on Beach Street, he passed the famous Buena Vista Café at the corner of Hyde. He almost felt like he could use one of their signature Irish coffees laced with Irish whiskey, right about now.

Joel glanced at his watch and hurried along the remaining couple of blocks back to his hotel.

* * * * * *

From his seat on the shuttle bus making its way from Fisherman's Wharf to the San Francisco Marriott, Joel looked out the window. Friday morning traffic in the city crawled along slowly. From high above the vehicles resembled ants squeezing through flagstones on a walkway.

As the bus headed down Columbus Avenue, the tip of the Transamerica pyramid sparkled in the sunlight on the horizon. The reflections from the tower danced right through the windshield, momentarily blinding riders now and then.

What a great city, he mused, as he recalled other visits he and Lora had made to the Bay Area for past ADA meetings and how much they had enjoyed themselves. Sure, there were sessions and other meetings to attend at the conference, but afterward they took time to be tourists.

That's how they rewarded themselves for the fruits of their hard work, building Joel's dental practice up from the early years. But now, the practice felt like nothing but a big burden.

"See someone you know?"

Perplexed, Joel turned and looked quizzically at the grinning man sitting next to him.

"I'm sorry?"

The man replied, "You were looking so intently out the window, I was wondering if there was someone you knew out there in the park." He gestured toward the window, as Washington Square Park and the Saints Peter and Paul Church came into view.

Joel grinned ruefully. "I'm sorry, I was just lost in thought. Didn't mean to be rude."

"No worries." The man extended his hand. "I'm Davis Avalon."

"Joel Chenoski." Joel shook Davis's hand firmly and noted the other man's neatly-fitting sport jacket, blue striped dress shirt, and only the suggestion of a spare tire at the waistband of his gray dress slacks.

"You're here for the ADA meeting, I presume?"

"Sure am," said Davis. "It's my first time coming to one of these. I thought I'd check one out sometime to see what it's like."

"They certainly do a good job putting these on," Joel admitted.

Davis shifted in his seat. "How about you? Your first time?"

"No." Joel shook his head. "I've been to these several times through the years." He paused and looked out the window again as the bus resumed its course.

"But it might be my last."

"Why do you say that?" Davis turned to look at his new acquaintance, surprised at the honesty.

"Well, that's a story I won't burden you with, but let's just say that the expense might not be the best use of my funds right now." Joel stared straight ahead at the back of the seat in front of him.

"It's definitely a splurge, with the conference fee, air, and the hotel," agreed Davis. "I thought I'd treat myself this year as a reward for having a decent year back at the office."

He continued, "But I also figured I'd save a little money by not staying at the conference hotel. I booked a room at the Holiday Inn Express and Suites, a couple of blocks from the Wharf."

Joel replied, "I'm at the Courtyard by the Wharf. How is your hotel? I was considering it when I made a reservation."

"It's fine. The room is pretty basic, but it's clean, and there's breakfast included." Davis took a sip from the coffee cup he held in his left hand. "Helps keep the travel costs under control, especially since my wife is here also."

"Where are you from?" Joel eyed Davis's coffee and wished that he hadn't downed the cup he bought from Ghirardelli Square so quickly.

"I live on Long Island, about 20 miles east of New York City." Davis drank the rest of his coffee. "Where do you live?"

"About 30 minutes outside of Denver." Joel thought for a moment. "So your wife came with you? What's she doing while you're at the meeting?"

Davis looked out the shuttle window as the San Francisco Marriott approached. "Malita – my wife – has a couple of college classmates who live in the Bay Area, so she's getting together with them."

He laughed. "Maybe doing some shopping or otherwise spending our practice's margin. But that's okay. Like I said, this is sort of a reward trip for us."

The shuttle bus came to a stop in front of the hotel entrance, and the passengers started to get up. As the men stood up, Joel said, "You said you had a good year? I've found things to be pretty flat where I am."

Davis motioned to Joel to go ahead of him. They moved to the front. "It was a good year, but not because we added a lot of new clients. We were just able to really connect with our current client base."

The men left the bus and walked into the hotel together. Suddenly Joel stopped and looked at Davis.

"Clients? What clients? You mean patients?"

Davis grinned. "Both. In my office, we refer to our patients as clients. I just prefer that my team think of them as clients."

Joel stared at him, uncomprehending, oblivious of the stream of attendees that parted around the two men partially blocking the doorway.

"I don't understand what you mean."

Davis looked around and realized they'd better get moving. He motioned to Joel as he turned, and walked through the doors into the hotel lobby. Inside, safely out of the path of foot traffic, Davis stopped and continued his explanation.

"I found that when we called them 'patients', my office team started to think of them as people who are patient. Like we can take our time doing anything for them, because they have patience."

Joel still had a puzzled look on his face as he tried to follow the words. Davis's grin grew wider as he kept talking.

"Get it? I mean they could end up thinking of them as people with p-a-t-i-e-n-c-e, not as p-a-t-i-e-n-t-s. And if you know someone is patient, then you might not naturally feel like you have to hurry for them, like you would if they were impatient."

Davis scanned the throng of attendees filing through the entrance. "Bottom line, Joel, we weren't valuing our clients' time. We were treating them like they should wait for us."

Joel's face cleared. "Got it. I thought you were trying to test me. But you're not trying to hurry people along, are you?"

"No, not at all, that's not the point." Davis hid his impatience from Joel. "I just want my office team to remember that our clients' time is valuable, and that we should treat them like we appreciate that fact."

He looked past the meeting attendees milling around the lobby, and craned his neck to see where they needed to go. "I've just seen it too many times, where in a dentist's or even a doctor's office, the staff thinks that patients should understand that the provider's time is what's important, because the provider's busy. And if the patient has to wait, she needs to understand that's the way it is.

"I even personally experienced this once – I took my daughter to a doctor's office, and saw a sign on the wall that read 'We are a busy office. You should expect to wait up to an hour for your appointment.'"

Davis raised his arms, palms up, and leaned forward toward the other man. "Can you believe that? So I asked the receptionist, what do you mean, if I have a 2 o'clock appointment, you already know in advance that I might have to wait until 3 o'clock?"

"What did she say?" asked Joel.

"Basically the same thing as the sign – they're a busy office, and you should expect to wait." Davis threw his hands up again. "Unbelievable. That tells you they overbook deliberately. That also tells you that's how little they care about their clients' time."

Exasperation written all over his face, he stabbed the air with his forefinger and looked at Joel. "I don't want that sort of thing happening in my office – that's why I have my team think of our patients as clients."

Joel nodded slowly as he absorbed what Davis had just told him, then almost jumped and looked at his watch. "Listen, I know the sessions are about to start, but I want to hear more about what you said about connecting with your patients. That is, if you don't mind."

"They're *clients*, Joel, start remembering that!" Davis admonished with a grin. "Well, let's plan on catching up at lunch or at the end of the day," said Davis. "Besides, it'll be good for me to hang out with you since I've never been to an ADA meeting, and you have. You could give me some tips!"

"Fair enough," said Joel. After comparing agendas and agreeing to meet up at lunchtime, the two men shook hands and went their separate ways.

SMILE!

"A smile is a curve that sets everything straight."
-- Phyllis Diller

The morning sessions went by quickly enough. The keynote was the usual keynote-sounding speech. The couple of breakout sessions that Joel attended afterward held his interest, though in the second one, "Cementation and Adhesion", his thoughts wandered back to the conversation he had with Davis earlier.

An interesting guy, he mused. The economy on Long Island must be better than it is in my part of Denver. Or maybe he does more advertising than I do, and brings in more through that. Maybe I need to put out more ads.

But I can't afford more advertising, he deliberated. I'm already paying my office staff more than their fair share, and that doesn't leave me much for other things.

By now Joel had tuned out the breakout session speaker as he became immersed in his thoughts once again. Only when everyone stood up to file out of the room, did he realize that the session was over.

As he followed the last of the attendees out, he complimented the speaker.

"Nice job, thank you!" Joel couldn't even recall what the speaker had said during the last half-hour.

Once in the hallway, he looked at his conference agenda where he'd made notes on which sessions he would attend. He realized he had another 45 minutes or so before it was time for lunch, so he decided to find a place to call his wife.

He spotted a chair in one corner of the second floor atrium, next to a window overlooking Mission Street, and plunked down into it. Joel pulled out his cell phone and speed-dialed his wife's phone.

"Hi Lora, it's me." His wife's voice always made him feel better.

"Hi honey, how's it going in San Francisco?"

"Pretty good. I'm sitting here looking out the window at a green park surrounded by buildings in the middle of the city." He had a view of Yerba Buena Gardens right through the spotless glass.

"How's the conference?"

Joel proceeded to tell Lora about the sessions and the hotel, then backtracked and told her about his thoughts during the morning while he was out for a walk.

"On the shuttle bus coming over here from the Courtyard, I met this interesting guy from Long Island. It's his first time at an annual meeting, and he said he was treating himself for having had a pretty good year. His wife is also here, but she's visiting old college roommates."

Joel felt a twinge of regret as he said it. That Lora was not there with him tugged on his conscience.

"So his practice is doing okay?" asked Lora.

"That's what he said," replied Joel. "But I'm going to catch up with him more, maybe at meal times, so I can hear more. He said something about revenues being up because he was able to make better connections with his patients."

Joel shifted in his chair and paused as several dentists walked by, talking loudly. "It'll be interesting to find out what he means."

"That would, honey, but doesn't it take more patients to get more revenue?"

"Well, that's what I thought." Joel looked out the window again. "Maybe if our office staff focused more on their jobs and less on bickering with each other, we'd get more people in." His voice started to take on a bit of a rant.

Lora just listened, as she always did when Joel's ranting moods appeared.

"Anyway, at least I don't have to ask how things are at the office, since it's Friday."

"Not only that," replied Lora, "but you're closed until you get back." She smiled into the phone.

"Oh yeah," said Joel sarcastically, "but we still have to pay the people. Oh well, it's what it is." Irritation started to well up again.

Knowing her husband's moods, Lora moved on. "What session are you going to attend next?" she asked evenly.

Joel looked at his watch. "I'm going to find Davis at lunch and try to sit with him, so I can continue our conversation. What are you going to do now?"

Lora gave him a short summary of her plans for the afternoon.

"Well honey, have a good afternoon then. I probably won't be able to call you again until after I get back to the hotel tonight, okay?"

"No problem, call when you can." The two said their goodbyes and ended the call.

Joel rose from the chair somewhat awkwardly and looked around for the ballroom where lunch was being served. His roving eyes stopped on the name over the door halfway down the hallway, and he headed in that direction.

"Hey Joel! How's it going?"

Joel turned to see Davis approaching, conference tote bag in hand.

"Hi Davis, how was your morning?" The two men entered the lunch room together.

"Pretty good." Davis was enthused. "I got a lot of good information and some things to think about that I might use in my practice."

Joel gestured to an empty table already set for lunch. "Want to start a new table?"

The dentists sat down next to each other. Taking his napkin and spreading it in his lap, Joel said to Davis,

"So what kinds of things did you hear about that were interesting?"

For the next several minutes, the two men traded highlights from the sessions they attended that morning. Their dialogue was occasionally interrupted by quick introductions as other people occupied the remaining seats at the lunch table.

After the lunch was officially kicked off by one of the organizers, with the lunch sponsor dutifully recognized, the level of noise in the room settled into the typical din of many simultaneous conversations taking place.

As he munched on a forkful of salad, Joel turned to Davis and said, "I'm interested in hearing more about what you said this morning."

"Fire away." Davis took a huge bite out of a roll. "What's on your mind?" he said. It sounded more like "Wafs on you minef?"

"Gosh, I don't know where to start." Joel shrugged and put his fork down. "All of what you mentioned got me thinking, so much so that I didn't even hear the last half-hour of the second session I went to."

Davis laughed, and stabbed at his salad with his fork as Joel continued.

"You mentioned that your revenues were up, but I think you said that wasn't because you had a lot of new patients, but because you made a better connection with your existing ones. Right?"

Davis nodded. "And remember, to us they're 'clients', not 'patients'."

Joel reached for a roll and gestured with it. "Right, got it. But how much advertising do you do to bring in new patien– uh, clients?"

Davis thought for a moment. "I do some advertising, but that's not really what's accounted for our growth last year." His eyes widened eagerly as a waiter placed his lunch plate in front of him and took the remnants of his salad away. "This looks good." He grinned at Joel.

"Dive in," encouraged Joel as his lunch plate appeared in front of him as well. He picked up a fork and said, "New patients – uh, clients" as Davis glared at him, "… are what grow revenue, so don't you use advertising for that?"

Davis put his fork down and sat back for a moment as his jaws worked on a mouthful of his lunch. After he swallowed, he said, "Okay so there's a fundamental concept that I'm going to talk about, that is probably contrary to most things you hear in our business."

He picked up his fork again and waved it in the air. "Lately I've been relying more on our clients to help bring us new business through referrals, rather than relying on ads to drive people to our office."

Davis sawed through a piece of chicken and continued. "Look at it this way. We're a service business … that is, we supply a service, right?"

Joel nodded, as he gave his lunch a little more of his attention.

"How likely would it be for you to go to a service provider, only because you saw their ad on TV?" asked Davis. "Probably not likely, right?"

Joel shrugged his shoulders and nodded again, mouth full of chicken.

"So I don't expect someone to see my ad once and think, 'I've just got to make Dr. Avalon my new dentist.' That's why I rely more on my current clients having such a great experience coming to my office, that they'll tell everyone they know that Dr. Avalon should be their dentist."

Davis's eyes zeroed in on his plate again, as he took another bite. "This is really pretty good!"

Joel found it amusing that the other man would enjoy his conference lunch so enthusiastically. There's nothing like having it all be new.

Staying on topic, Davis said, "So while everyone – well not everyone, but most people in our business, obsesses about whether they're advertising enough to bring in new clients, I decided to focus on making the office experience so awesome that our clients wouldn't be able to help themselves but tell others about it."

He tapped Joel on the shoulder and pointed. "Can you pass the pepper? And that's how we try to grow our client base." Davis energetically ground more pepper onto his food.

Joel thought about what he just heard. "That sounds reasonable, but I've got problems with my office staff. I wouldn't call them 'awesome' right now. You're fortunate that you have the right people." He felt a tad bit envious.

Davis had almost completed his mission of clearing his plate. "It wasn't always that way. I had to figure out a way to give them an opportunity to be successful, a way where they could work more like a team. It was only then did I start to see results."

He lined up his fork and knife neatly on the now-empty plate. Joel looked down at it and could not locate even a speck of food remaining.

He grinned at Davis and nodded in the plate's direction. "Was that any good?"

"Nah. Think I'll send it back." Davis wiped his mouth with his napkin.

He returned to their topic of discussion. "I ended up creating a system, a framework, and made up a name for it so I could remember it more easily. I called it SMILE." He looked at Joel, with an expectant look on his face.

"SMILE?" asked Joel. "What does that mean?"

Davis leaned back as the waiter took his empty plate and replaced it with a smaller one containing a luscious-looking dessert.

"SMILE is an acronym." As he eyed his dessert appreciatively, Davis reached into his wallet and pulled out a small card. "Here's what it stands for." He passed it to Joel.

Joel looked at the card and read:

SMILE!

S = Simple

M = Manage

I = Initiative

L = Loyalty

E = Equip

"This is your system?" asked Joel, as the waiter placed a dessert in front of him too.

"Well, it's not a system, but I guess it's more of a framework of how I work with my office team. It helps me be sure that we're all in the right frame of mind to give the client an awesome experience, being our client." Davis picked up a clean fork and attacked his dessert with gusto.

Joel looked at the card. "When you figured this out, were you able to do this with the people you already had, or did you have to find new people?"

Davis nodded and replied, "Both. Those that were able to adapt and change, stayed on. I did have to let a couple of people go, unfortunately." He took another bite, and pointed to his now half-empty plate with his fork. "This is really good!"

His own dessert forgotten at the moment, Joel continued to study the card. He seemed to hesitate, then turned to Davis and said, "Is there any way I can have some of your time during the conference, to learn more about your SMILE framework?"

Davis put his fork down and thought for a moment. "Tell you what, since you've been to these meetings before ... I'll agree to tell you about SMILE, if we talk about it over food and you show me some of the great places to eat here in San Francisco. Does that sound fair?"

"Fair enough." Joel stuck out his hand and they shook on the deal.

"Hey, are you going to eat your dessert?"

Summary – SMILE!

SMILE is a framework for concepts and philosophies that you can use as an owner-dentist to apply your strategy to grow your practice. When consistently implemented, it can also empower your office team to participate in generating more revenues and profits for your business.

Since you're the owner-dentist, you still have to supply the strategy. SMILE is a tool you can use to implement your strategy synergistically with your office team, empowering them to become revenue generators too.

S = Simple

M = Manage

I = Initiative

L = Loyalty

E = Equip

Much more to come in the following pages!

"S" = Simple

"In thinking, keep to the simple."

-- Lao Tzu

The rest of the afternoon passed quickly enough for Joel. He tried to concentrate on the sessions he attended, because they did have some information he was interested in. The last workshop of the afternoon, "The Future of Dentistry", gave him some things to think about. But every now and then his mind wandered back to his conversation with Davis and the SMILE framework.

The method definitely caught his attention. Joel felt he was at the end of his rope with his office staff and their generally dysfunctional behavior. He had reached a point of not knowing what to do. It's not like he could fire all of them and begin again.

Davis's SMILE concept sounded like it could offer a solution, or at least give Joel something to think about.

Back in his hotel room at the Courtyard, Joel changed into a pair of jeans and a long sleeve polo. Putting a vest over that, he grabbed his windbreaker as he headed out the door. Evenings in San Francisco were always unpredictable. One minute the temperature was fine, the next minute the fog would roll in and you would freeze your tush off.

The men had agreed to meet in Joel's hotel lobby at 6:00 p.m., so he took the stairs down to the first floor and made his way to the front. When he reached the lobby, he saw Davis sitting in a chair looking at a Red and White Fleet brochure.

"Thinking of taking a cruise?" Joel smiled as he approached Davis's chair.

Davis looked up. "Have you ever been on one of these?"

"Lora – my wife – and I did the Bay Cruise once. It takes you out under the Golden Gate, and cruises between Alcatraz and Angel Island. The scenery was incredible, but I couldn't believe how windy it was!"

Davis stuffed the brochure into his jacket pocket as he stood up. "My wife and I are staying a couple of extra days after the conference, so maybe we'll give it a try."

The dentists walked out through the main door onto the sidewalk along Beach Street. Davis turned to Joel.

"Where to?"

"What do you feel like eating?" asked Joel as he stopped short, almost colliding with someone walking quickly by.

"Well, we're trading information for experience, here." Davis grinned as he scissored his hands back and forth between them, imitating an exchange. "I tell you about SMILE, and you show me the places to eat. So, you pick."

Joel stroked his chin for a moment and glanced at Davis sideways. "Do you like fresh seafood?"

"Love it, when I can get it."

"Let's walk this way a couple of blocks to Taylor, then to the Wharf." Joel gestured and started to walk.

As he fell in step with his new friend, Davis said, "For my part now, let's start with the S in SMILE. It relates to the business strategy for my practice, though the S doesn't stand for strategy. Did you have any guesses on what I mean by S for simple?"

Joel looked straight ahead as he walked, brows knit slightly. His expression cleared and he shrugged. "Keep it simple?"

"That's pretty much it. I found by trial and error, and all of the mistakes I made in the early going, that I had to get my team to understand my strategy for my practice in simple terms."

He turned toward Joel as he walked. "It's not that my staff isn't smart or they're not capable of understanding. It's just that I'd have all these great ideas of what we should be doing, telling them all about it, and then just confusing them."

"Turn left here," said Joel as they reached Taylor Street. "So were your people too confused to know what you wanted them to do next?"

"Sort of." Davis dodged a parking meter he almost walked into after turning the corner. "I was just throwing out ideas or visions of what I wanted to have happen, like saying 'let's figure out a way to get as many clients in as possible', but not having any idea of how to do that. That's not a strategy.

"You know, Joel, I thought I was – to use a popular word – 'empowering' them to do what they thought should be done. But actually I gave very little direction, and as you just pointed out, they weren't sure what I wanted them to do."

Davis stopped in mid-stride, arms akimbo, and said, "So they ended up doing a lot of different things, and not accomplishing much of anything." He threw up his hands. "They were working hard, but not working smart."

Joel had continued a few steps before he realized that Davis had stopped. He turned around. "That doesn't sound very productive."

The men resumed their pace, as they neared the corner at Jefferson Street. At that point, they could hear some of the racket coming from the Ripley's Believe It or Not place a couple of doors down.

"No, it wasn't," replied Davis. "And I was starting to get regularly irritated by it, thinking 'why don't you do what you're supposed to do to grow this practice?'.

"By the way, where are we going anyway, Alioto's?" He gestured at the legendary restaurant on their left as it came into view.

"No, I'm going to take you to a place I personally like a little better because it has a nicer view," Joel said. They turned the corner onto Embarcadero North and he pointed.

"Over there – The Franciscan Crab." The men headed for the entrance and started up the stairs. Davis paused to look at some of the many framed photos lining the walls.

"Hey, there's Lucille Ball! And Frank Sinatra. Did they all come here?"

Joel grinned. "I suppose. But whether they did or not, the food's still pretty good."

At the top of the stairs, the wait wasn't too bad, and in a short while the two were shown to a table next to the expansive floor-to-ceiling windows.

Davis sat down, his head on a swivel. "You were right, what a view!" he gushed. He sat for a moment, admiring the sights of the Golden Gate Bridge to the left and Alcatraz straight ahead, with Sausalito and Tiburon in the distance at the edge of the shimmering waters of the Bay.

"So, back to your S for simple," said Joel, as he unfolded his napkin and spread it on his lap. "I get that you want to keep things simple, but it's not like you can sit there and tell your staff every single thing that you want them to do."

He took a sip of water from his glass and continued. "That's how I feel sometimes with my staff – that I have to tell them everything or they won't necessarily do it."

Davis put down his menu and looked out the window again. "You're right, you can't do that. But that's not what I meant."

He turned back to Joel. "What I learned that I needed to do – or actually, what I needed to learn to do back then, was to figure out three or four things that my office team could live by. Three or four things that were easy to remember, and that most of the things that happen in a day would fall under." He looked up as a waiter approached the table.

After the server put a bread basket on their table and took their drink orders, Joel resumed the topic and asked, "What do you mean, 'most of the things that happen in a day would fall under'?"

"I mean three or four things they can remember that create rules for how they act, as they go through the day." Davis reached for a piece of bread and buttered it.

Joel shook his head. "I'm still not getting you."

The other dentist took a bite before answering. His eyes widened. "Hey, this is real sourdough! I love this stuff. I can't get this at home."

Amused by his new friend's epicurean enthusiasm, Joel replied, "Yes it is. And you're right, it's hard to get anything like it unless you're here in the Bay Area."

He paused, an expression of mock exasperation on his face. "*Now* will you tell me how the three or four things work?"

Davis nodded as he polished off the last of the bread slice and in the same motion reached for another. "Let me just tell you what I did, like I said, after some amount of trial and error.

"I came up with four things that I wanted my office team to always keep in mind as they went through their day. They were guidelines, thoughts that I wanted to help guide how they went about their work and how they interacted with clients through the day."

Their waiter arrived with their drink orders, but left again when the men said they needed more time to decide.

"All right, hold that thought," said Joel, "because we probably should figure out what we're going to have."

"Do you have any recommendations?" asked the dentist from Long Island.

"Well," Joel replied, "I'm almost certain you don't get much Dungeness crab on Long Island, so that's what I'd suggest. My wife goes crazy over it whenever we're here." He felt a pang of regret again, with Lora having to stay home.

"I love crab, so I'll go with your call." Davis looked over the menu one last time, then closed it and nodded at Joel.

"What are you having? And did you say your wife couldn't join you this trip?"

Joel looked out the window at the passengers down below on the sidewalk, standing in line for the next Red and White Fleet cruise departure. "No, we decided that we shouldn't spend the extra money for her to come out too. I had already registered and paid for the meeting before we made that decision."

He looked up at Davis, eyes narrowed with tension. "You see, that's the problem I'm struggling with right now. And that's why I appreciate being able to pick your brain for a little bit."

Joel took a sip of his drink, and continued. "My office staff has been a drain on me lately. They've been really reminding me that they're an expense. And over the past couple of years, while my revenues have been flat, that expense keeps increasing."

"Why does it keep increasing?"

"Well, people expect raises, don't they, so I can keep them on," Joel replied.

He took an even bigger swig of his drink. "Lately, I really have not known what to do about it. They should be doing more, but like I said, I can't tell them every single thing to do, every moment of the day. I'm busy bringing in the revenue, helping patients."

Davis listened thoughtfully. "They're 'clients', by the way." He nodded. "I get it. You feel like you're in a corner. Revenues are not great, your office staff acts like they're not motivated, yet you have to keep them on. Right?"

"Right."

"That's why I think SMILE can work for you." Davis stared for a moment at the view outside, beyond the wall of windows. He suddenly turned back to Joel and pointed at him.

"And once you figure out how to apply SMILE to your practice, you'll either be able to see if you have the right people on your team, or you'll make sure you get the right people."

Out of nowhere the waiter appeared at a corner of their table. "Are you ready to order?"

"Yes!" Davis picked up his menu again, and said, "I'll start with a bowl of clam chowder, then have a half-order of roasted Dungeness crab."

"Very good, sir." The waiter looked at Joel. "And you, sir?"

"I'll also start with a bowl of chowder, and then the Crab Louie."

"The crab, or clam chowder, sir?"

"Clam, please."

The waiter gathered up the menus and left. Davis continued. "So back to the four things I mentioned for my office ... here's what I have them keep in mind."

He turned his chair slightly in Joel's direction, leaned back, and crossed his legs. "First thing, I want them to keep in mind whatever they can do to create loyalty from our client. I ask my team, 'What can you do today that will create loyalty on the part of our clients due to our exceptional service?' I want them to remember that – always try to be exceptional with our service."

Their chowders arrived. Davis sat up and pulled his chair in as he examined his soup with anticipation. Spoon in hand, he dipped it into the bowl, raised a taste to his lips and rolled his eyes.

"Unbelievable!"

Joel grinned. "I'm glad you like it." The man from Long Island had no end to his appreciation for good food.

Davis continued as he tackled his chowder. "Item number two – I want us as an office to provide technical excellence in all of the procedures that we do for our clients. We need to be good with the technology that we use in our office."

"By technology, do you mean computers and such?" said Joel. He rested his spoon in his soup bowl and dabbed at his lips with his napkin.

"Not just the computer system, but also any other technology we might use, like digital radiography, VELscope, CEREC, The Wand, GALILEOS, DIAGNodent … whatever."

"Do you use all those?"

"Not all of them." Davis scraped the side of his soup bowl with his spoon. "I was just saying that whatever technology we've got in the office, we should have technical excellence when using it. For example, we shouldn't be fumbling around with bite wings in the client's mouth. We should be able to handle them quickly and expertly."

He laid the spoon down next to the empty bowl as he scanned for any remnants of chowder. Davis looked up at Joel again as something occurred to him.

"Oh, and that excellence with technology should include using our administrative systems too."

"The back office stuff?" asked Joel, eyebrows raised inquisitively.

"That's a common term that I don't really think is accurate," replied Davis. "When you think about it, it's not really 'back office'. Our admin systems affect our clients one way or another. 'Back office' to me sounds like there's no effect on them."

Joel just looked at Davis as he tried to comprehend his latest point.

Davis continued, "Don't you see? The admin systems, like our claims submission function, our electronic appointment reminder system, and our practice management system overall, help make our services affordable to our clients."

He took a drink of water. "Without those, we wouldn't be able to serve our clients as well, because we'd be spending too much time and energy just trying to manage our business."

Davis put his water glass back down. "If nothing else, they should be called 'front office' systems."

Joel's face cleared a little. "I think I see what you're getting at. You're saying that our staff members need to be able to use those technologies well too, to help keep the office running smoothly."

Davis nodded and pointed emphatically at Joel's chest. "Absolutely right. Remember, the smoother running the front office, the better the client experience."

Joel wiped his mouth with his napkin. "Okay, so that's two things. What are the other two?"

"Number three, we want to be punctual and efficient, so our clients don't have to come in more often than necessary." Davis reached for yet another slice of the sourdough bread. He buttered it and took a bite before continuing.

"And when they do come in, we make sure we see them on time, and keep them on time. We want them to feel like we know their time is valuable, too."

Davis swallowed and looked at Joel. "You know, I'm *really* enjoying this bread."

Joel nodded, engrossed in the train of thought. "So you don't want your clients feeling like you did when you took your kid to that doctor's office?"

"Right, nothing like that should happen in my office."

A busboy came by and picked up their empty soup bowls. Joel moved on. "All right that's number three. What's the last one?"

"Number four, we want to make any contact between us and our clients an overall pleasant experience for them. That includes not only face-to-face in the office, but also over the phone if they call us." Davis finished off his drink and waved his empty glass as he continued speaking.

"Too many of us in our business are so busy with the technical details, that sometimes we might forget that there's a client sitting there with her mouth wide open. I wanted my office team to try and not forget that."

Joel smiled. "Well, you can't help it if the patien – *client* is going to have pain, or is afraid of pain, so sometimes we have to get technical." He corrected himself before Davis could yell at him.

"Right," Davis agreed. "But how we treat them as a client – as a person – can go a long way toward minimizing that pain or the fear of the unknown. If one of my team members is having a bad day and she decides to take it out on our client, that won't help soothe any fears."

Joel nodded absently as he gazed out the window, oblivious for the moment to the gorgeous view. "Good point."

The men were silent for a moment. Joel continued to stare out the window in thought. Again out of nowhere, the waiter suddenly appeared holding their dinners.

Back in focus, Joel noticed with amusement that Davis's eyes widened with hungry anticipation as the server placed his half-order of crab in front of him. Joel's crab louie looked nothing short of humongous.

"Anything else I can bring you right now, gentlemen?" As each man shook his head, the waiter withdrew. "Enjoy."

Joel gestured toward his friend's plate. "Let's enjoy our food for a bit. I'll give you a chance to eat." Davis needed no further encouragement as he picked up a crab leg and got busy with his crab cracker.

For the next few minutes, both men concentrated on their dishes, with little conversation except the occasional reverent sounds Davis made as he enjoyed the flavors of his food. He looked up from his crab cracking over at Joel.

"How's your salad?"

Joel, in the midst of enjoying his own meal and also the sight of Davis clearly relishing his, replied, "Great. How's your dinner?"

Davis's mouth was full as he nodded and gave two thumbs up. He reached for another piece of sourdough.

Joel waited until there was a point where Davis seemed to take a breath, then returned to the topic at hand.

"So those four things you mentioned, helped your staff in their daily work?"

Davis nodded, as he placed his napkin in his lap and sat back for a moment. "When you think about it, if they can remember all four things, that gives them guidance on the important things to keep in mind, and how they should go about their day."

He took a drink from his water glass and continued. "Let's take number one, 'do that exceptional thing that creates loyalty from our clients'. I want my team to remember to do exceptional things. Not just average. And certainly not sub-standard, because they happen to be having a bad day."

"And do they remember?" asked Joel.

"I hope so. At least, we review these four things enough times so I hope it's something they can remember on a regular basis."

Davis picked up his crab cracker again and started to reach for another leg, but paused. "Let's try out number two, about providing 'technical excellence'. Like I said before, all of us need to be very good, but hopefully excellent with any technology we use in the office. Especially the technology we use on our patients."

Joel nodded in agreement. Davis grabbed a crab leg and said with a grin, "After all, if you were a client, you wouldn't want to see us fumbling around with our technology, then ask you to open wide, would you?"

"No, that wouldn't be good." Joel shook his head. "I had something like that happen to me a long time ago, when I was having a tooth extracted."

Davis cracked away at the crab leg as Joel continued his story.

"The dentist who extracted my tooth was good, but he had a new assistant who had just been trained as a dental assistant, after being in some other industry like manufacturing for her whole career.

"I'm not necessarily against that type of situation, but the assistant, who was supposed to be using the suction, poked me repeatedly in the cheek and tongue with the tip. She kept looking away to see what the dentist was doing, and wasn't holding the suction still."

Davis grinned. "That must have been annoying."

"To say the least. When the dentist called me later that night to see how I was doing, I gave him the feedback then. He apologized and said he'd talk to her."

Davis continued with his point. "So if my team remembers that we have to show technical excellence, then hopefully they remember that they've got to be good with any technology we use on our clients, even with something as basic as an aspirator."

Joel finished off his crab louie and put his fork down on the empty plate.

"So let me see if I get this one straight." Joel steepled his fingers as he thought. "Number three for your office was to be on time and efficient, so you don't delay your patients, and they don't have to come in any more often than necessary."

"You've got that right." Davis pointed his crab cracker at Joel. "Except they're *clients*, not patients. Remember?" He winked.

"Guilty as charged." Joel held up his hands. "And if your staff keeps this in mind, your *clients* feel like you value their time? Unlike the doctor's office where you took your kid?"

"Right again. We want them to feel like we appreciate them taking the time to be in our office." Davis picked through the last of the crab shells to be sure he'd found every edible morsel.

He put down his fork. "Mind you, we don't apologize for taking their time – unless we somehow made them wait longer than they should. But whatever time it takes, it takes, assuming we've done our jobs right. We just want them to know, that *we* know they're taking time out of their day to go to the dentist."

Just then the waiter reappeared, cleared their plates, and asked if there was anything else he could offer.

"How about a dessert menu?" suggested Joel, as he looked at his guest with mock curiosity. "You eat dessert, don't you Davis?"

After the server left, Joel continued, "And for your fourth item, how you want your office staff to make any contact a pleasant experience for your clients. I'm thinking that with this item, if they're having a bad day, you want them to leave that at home?"

"Absolutely. Clients don't really care if you're having a bad day, and they won't give you any free passes because you spilled coffee on yourself at home that morning."

Davis looked out the windows as the mellow tones of twilight started to settle on the scenic view. "As I tend to say, clients just want to be customers. They don't want to know all the difficulties you're having today."

He turned back to Joel. "So you see how the 'S' works? You pick a small number of high-level things for your office team to focus on. This composes your strategy of sorts. If you pick the right items, and your people internalize them, those strategy items help guide your team's daily activities and how they perform them.

"The strategic item has to be specific enough so they know what it means to them, yet it must be high-level enough so it can serve as a guide for how they act."

Davis warmed to his point and was on a roll. "It can't be some high-level thing like 'get as many new clients as possible'. That's not specific enough. The team won't know what to do with that item."

He shifted his chair a little closer to the table as he saw the waiter approaching from across the dining room. "But an action item like 'make it a pleasant experience for the client' is something that everyone can intuitively understand, and general enough to serve as a guide for their behavior.

"And that's how I don't have to tell them exactly what I want them to do." Davis looked up as the waiter arrived at their table. "Don't forget, the S is for Simple. It's got to be easy to remember."

"Dessert menus, gentlemen," said the server. Davis started studying the short menu quickly.

"Just a decaf for me," said Joel. "Davis, you get whatever looks good to you."

Davis had that wide-eyed expression again as he checked out the selections. He handed his menu back to the waiter. "I'll have the Monterosa Wild Strawberry Italian Cheesecake. And a regular coffee."

He looked at Joel as the server withdrew. "Are you good with the S in SMILE now? Does it make sense?"

"I think so." Joel nodded with satisfaction. "You've done a great job explaining it. Now I see how you can create these simple strategy items that can serve as almost a guiding light for your office staff. I'll have to give some thought to what those would be for my office."

The waiter returned with their coffees and Davis's cheesecake. For the rest of the meal, the two men engaged in talk about other topics, and learned more about each other's families.

At the conclusion of dinner, dessert plate and coffee cup empty, Davis declared, "Now *that* was awesome."

"Glad you liked it." Joel smiled. For the past two hours, there had been no doubt that Davis was anywhere but in food heaven.

Joel settled the check, over Davis's politely insistent objections. The men stood up and headed toward the stairs back to street level.

On their return stroll to their hotels from The Franciscan Restaurant, they arrived at the Courtyard first.

"I leave you at this point," said Joel, as he extended his hand. "Dr. Avalon, it was a pleasure getting to know you today."

"Well, *Dr.* Chenoski, the pleasure was mine, and thank you again for dinner. You really didn't have to treat, you know." Davis shook his host's hand.

Joel waved dismissively. "Really, it's the least I could do, after I picked your brain tonight. And that was only the first letter of the five in SMILE!"

"Well, for the next letter 'M', tomorrow's dinner is on me. Remember that," admonished Davis. "See you in the morning."

Summary – "S" = Simple

Your objectives for your practice must be stated simply and clearly, so your office team can quickly understand what you aspire to do. They also need to be able to remember your objectives easily.

• Decide on your strategy for your practice. What's most important to you? How do you want to be known by your clients?

• Formulate your major strategic objectives, 3 or 4 at the most.

• Be sure they are simple enough to be easily understood.

• Be sure they are also simple enough to be easily explained and remembered.

• Selecting the appropriate strategy items helps guide office team's daily behavior and decision making.

Think strategically first, to more effectively compose your strategic objectives. Properly formulated, your strategy items create a "guiding light" for your office team members.

"M" = Manage

"The way management treats associates is exactly how the associates will treat the customers."

-- Sam Walton

Day two of the ADA conference seemed to drag on for Joel. It was only mid-morning, but to him it felt like the middle of the afternoon. He fidgeted in the session room, trying his best to concentrate on the techniques of using some new laser technology to treat peri-implantitis. But his thoughts kept straying back to the conversation he had with his wife earlier that morning.

"Hi honey, it's me." Joel called her at 6:00 in the morning, while he was still in bed.

"Hi dear, are you up already?" Lora, one hour ahead in Denver, had just finished her morning workout and was standing in the kitchen.

"Getting there. Thought I'd call you since I didn't get to last night. I was afraid I might wake you."

"That's what I figured. How was dinner last night?" Lora poured herself a cup of coffee and went to the fridge for the cream, phone trapped between her shoulder and her ear.

"It was great." Joel stretched and yawned. He told her about where he and Davis went, what they had, and what they talked about.

"He really opened my eyes with his SMILE framework. Last night he gave me the overview of the

S, which means simple, referring to the business strategy for the practice."

"Do you think some of that might apply to your practice?" asked Lora, as she sipped her hot coffee carefully, steam rising into her eyes.

"I think so. I'll have to think more about it, and want to ask you what you think too." Joel sat up and swung his legs out of bed, facing the wall. "Remember how I was telling you that I wasn't sure what to do about our office staff, how I should handle them?"

He stood up and stretched. "I was at wit's end, mad at them for not doing their jobs as well as they should, having a bad attitude – yet I was afraid I might lose them."

Joel started to pace the room as he continued. "The conversation I had last night with Davis gave me some hope that you and I can figure this out. He was in a similar situation with his staff a couple of years ago. And now he's attending this conference with his wife as a reward for having a good year!"

"Did he say what he changed to get that improvement in his business?" Lora, concentrating, stared at the fall colors outside their kitchen window.

"I'll tell you more when I get home, but the gist of the S in SMILE is that he was at first getting too complicated with his strategy. When he tried to communicate that to his staff, they didn't know what he was talking about."

Joel took a break from his pacing and sat down in the desk chair. "It wasn't necessarily their fault that they didn't understand what Davis wanted. He wasn't being clear. He didn't make it simple enough, so that's why the S is for simple."

Lora could hear her husband's energy in his voice as he recapped the previous evening. "Sounds like you had a good discussion, dear."

"Absolutely. I can't wait to hear more about the other letters in SMILE." He drummed his fingers impatiently on the desk and sighed. "Maybe this could be a turning point in our trying to figure out what to do.

"I only wish you could be here too," he added wistfully.

"Me too, dear," said Lora. "But we agreed that we should save the money."

Joel jolted back to reality as people in his session started to get up and leave. He had daydreamed his way to the end of the breakout again, and honestly couldn't recall the last ten minutes of what the speaker said.

He rose and started to follow everyone else out. As he passed the session speaker, Joel called out, "Nice job, thank you!" Maybe he could read the conference proceedings to catch up on what he missed.

Once in the hallway, he headed down to the registration area to check the board for the latest changes and additions. As he studied the posted changes and compared them to his conference program, he heard his name called.

"Hey Joel, how are you doing?"

Joel turned just as Davis approached, and said, "Davis! How are you today?"

They shook hands. Chuckling as he rubbed his belly, Davis replied, "Just great. I think I'm still full from last night's dinner!"

Joel grinned. The image of Davis enjoying himself immensely was still fresh in his mind.

"How is your day going?" Davis nodded at the agenda that Joel was holding.

"Good. I'm catching some of the sessions that I wanted to." Joel left out the fact that he'd not been listening very closely during. "How about you?"

"Same. I went to an interesting workshop on occlusal equilibration." He looked around quickly and lowered his voice conspiratorially. "Some of the other sessions are kind of dry, though. Had to bring in an extra cup of coffee."

Joel laughed. "I know what you mean. Say, what's your wife up to today?"

"She's getting together with another one of her old roommates. I think someone who lives in the South Bay … I want to say Palo Alto?"

Joel thought for a moment. "I think 'South Bay' refers more to the San Jose and Santa Clara area, like where the 49ers play at Levi Stadium. Palo Alto is more what people call 'the peninsula'. But who knows." He shrugged, palms upturned.

Davis nodded. "Anyway, somewhere about 30 to 40 minutes from here. She and her girlfriend were going to meet for lunch, then probably hang out all the way through dinner."

"So, do you have time for dinner tonight?" Joel asked hopefully.

"Absolutely! I was looking forward to getting together with my culinary guide again." Davis laughed heartily.

The dentists decided to meet at Davis's hotel that evening, then go from there.

* * * * * *

Joel strode purposefully into the lobby of the Holiday Inn Express and Suites, taking the main door facing North Point Street. He was a few minutes early. Spotting an empty chair in the lobby, he walked over and sat down.

His smartphone vibrated in his pocket. A quick look told him that Lora had texted. After he turned his phone horizontally so the keyboard keys were larger, he typed a reply and sent it, telling her he was about to head out to dinner with Davis.

"Ah, there you are Joel," said Davis as he walked up to the chair. Joel put his phone away and stood up.

After they shook hands, Davis said, "Where are we headed tonight? I'm getting hungry."

Joel began to wonder if Davis was ever *not* hungry. "Well, if you're up for it, we'll go to one of the best places in the city for prime rib, if that's something you eat. Do you?"

"I think you can read my mind!" Davis exclaimed. "Last night's seafood was really great, of course, but today I was thinking I wouldn't mind some meat and potatoes. Whereabouts?"

"The House of Prime Rib," replied Joel, as he headed toward the front door of the hotel. "But I think we might take a cab. It's a pretty long walk."

"I don't mind the walk," offered Davis brightly. "How long are we talking about?"

"Probably a half an hour or more. It's on Van Ness Avenue. I don't think I feel like working that hard for dinner. Besides, I called for a reservation before I came over here."

"That works." Davis started looking for a cruising cab. "I didn't realize it was that far."

Before long the men flagged down a cab and jumped in. As it pulled away from the curb, Davis said to Joel, "You made a reservation, then?"

"Yes, I took a chance and called them from the hotel. Usually it's pretty hard to get in, but tonight there were some cancellations, so I was able to get something." Joel shifted in his seat and watched the buildings pass as they rode down North Point toward Van Ness Avenue. A block before Van Ness the driver made a left onto Polk and headed south.

"Wasn't that Van Ness down there?" asked Davis, He had seen the street sign before the cab turned.

"He's going down this street so we'll come out on Van Ness and be on the same side as the restaurant. Otherwise we'd have to do a U-turn, and sometimes that's tricky."

Davis looked at his colleague in admiration. "You really know your way around, do you."

Joel shrugged. "Like I told you, I've been here a few times before." He paused in mock drama. "But maybe this is the last."

"Knock it off," said Davis, in a stern but similarly mock tone. "Besides, tonight's topic is the M in SMILE, so maybe you'll start to see the possibilities of the mindset."

"I already see the possibilities." Joel told Davis about the conversation he had with his wife in the morning. "That's why I'm eager to find out the rest, and figure out how I might apply it to my problems."

The taxi pulled up in front of the restaurant. Joel paid the driver and Davis got out, taking in the sight of the bright neon sign "House of Prime Rib", with the words again repeated on the wall of the building over the long red awning. Old-English style white letters on the awning read "Est. 1949".

Joel held the restaurant door open for Davis. "After you!"

Inside, Joel checked in at the hostess podium and was told it would be about 5 minutes. He walked back to where Davis stood, eyes roving the dining room.

Fixed on a point about halfway into the room, Davis said, "This is amazing. Take a look at the size of that cart there with all the prime rib inside!"

In the middle of the room a man in a white chef's jacket and a chef's hat stood tall, carving prime rib from a roast inside a huge silver rolling cart. The gleaming cart's dome lid was open, and lights inside the dome illuminated a cutting board along with several large roasts standing up like tree trunks in a forest.

"The prime rib is definitely amazing," admitted Joel. "I think you'll really like it here." I know for sure you'll like it here, he thought.

"It's certainly a change of pace from last night," observed the dentist from Long Island. "Last night we had quite a view, but tonight ..." He looked around. "... No windows at all."

The restaurant indeed was windowless other than the front door. It had the look of an old-fashioned steak house with overstuffed chairs, dark wood on the walls, and lots of wall hangings or rows of books in bookcases. Chandeliers or bowl light fixtures hung from the ceiling.

"You definitely come here for the food and not for the view," agreed Joel. "But I think the ambience fits the menu quite well."

"Anyway, while we're waiting, back to the M in SMILE." Davis looked away from the bustle of the dining room and returned his gaze to Joel. "You know from the card I gave you that the M stands for manage, but do you have any thoughts on what I mean by that?"

The other dentist thought for a moment. "This is where I wasn't sure. Last night we talked about not wanting to be in a position where you have to tell people what to do all the time."

Joel stroked his chin in thought then continued. "Yet, the word 'manage' has some amount of telling people what to do in it. So I'm guessing you have to do some of it, but maybe not overdo it ... ?"

"Actually, that's not too far from it." Davis nodded. "As I found out – again the hard way – no matter how good your office team is, they're not always in a position to be self-directed. The simple strategy items alone from the 'S' are not going to do it."

An attractive young woman walked up to the men and said, "Dr. Chenosky? Your table is now ready." The dentists followed as she led them to their table in another room.

Davis sat down and looked at the surroundings. "It's like being in a little library here!"

Joel accepted the menu from the hostess. "I like this room. It doesn't get the hustle and bustle some of the other rooms get." He leaned forward to continue the previous thought.

"So if the 'S' items alone aren't going to do it, you still have to manage the staff somewhat, right?"

"Right." Davis nodded and rested his folded arms over the menu laying on the table in front of him. "But you have to strike the right balance. Micromanage people, and you spend all your time doing that and probably irritate them too. If you don't manage enough, things could get out of hand before you can take control."

Davis sat back and picked up his menu. "And it depends on the type of people you have on your team, as you already know. Some folks have more initiative than others."

A busboy appeared at their table, poured ice water for each of them, then left a basket of bread and a plate of butter. Davis leaned forward, lifting the end of the napkin covering the basket.

"Hey, is that sourdough?" He eyed the slices hungrily.

"It is," replied Joel, "but it's not quite as flavorful as the bread we had on the Wharf. I'm never sure why. But this is still pretty good."

Davis took a slice, helped himself to butter, then took a bite. "Tastes just as good to me." He looked into the basket again and pointed. "What's that?"

Joel used his clean fork to spear what Davis indicated, and put it on his colleague's plate. "These are cornbread sticks. Try one."

Davis tried it, nodded his head and gave a thumbs up.

"So the gist of the M is to manage the staff enough, but not to micromanage." Joel rubbed his chin again. "I thought I'd been doing some of that already, but still not getting results."

"Can you give me an example?" Davis had changed his gastronomic focus to the cornbread sticks.

"Well, my office manager is someone who's been with me for a long time, since my early years as I was building my practice." Joel picked a cornbread stick for himself – better get one before Davis devoured them all.

"She has a number of responsibilities," Joel continued. "Lately, though, I've been having a more difficult time finding out the status of whatever it is she's working on."

Davis nodded, taking a sip from his water glass.

Joel took a bite of his cornbread, pausing in thought. "Here's an example. Susan – my office manager – was doing the marketing for the practice. We'd talk about placing certain ads, or creating a take-home piece for our patients that would help them keep us in mind."

He took a drink of water and went on. "The work wasn't getting done, and I was having a hard time getting an answer about where it stood. Susan would get defensive and say it wasn't done because she got busy with the accounting, or busy with updating the computer, or something else."

Joel started to get irritated from telling the story. "And when I'd ask her when she thought she'd be done with say, the take-home piece, she'd give me some vague answer in a tone of voice that somehow told me to mind my own business."

As he sat back and glared right at Davis across the table, Joel declared, "That was a time where I made myself mad more than anyone else. I'm thinking, I'm the business owner, I deserve to know what's going on. Yet, I didn't know how to bring myself to say it."

He stared at his fingers drumming on the table for a moment as he paused and took a deep breath. Joel concluded, "Maybe deep down I didn't want to lose Susan, who'd been with me for so many years. She helped me get to where I was at that point."

Then he looked up again. "But come to think of it, perhaps I wasn't realizing – until maybe now – that Susan had already reached the limit of her abilities."

Joel reached into the basket for a slice of bread and buttered it. "It irritated me that I'd walk away frustrated and say nothing." He pointed at Davis. "After this trip, no more."

Just then a waiter sidled up to the table.

"Good evening, gentlemen, welcome to The House of Prime Rib. Have you been here before?"

"Well, he has," replied Davis, pointing to his dinner companion.

"Excellent, then perhaps you already know that dinners include our famous spinning salad, mashed or baked potato, Yorkshire pudding, and creamed spinach."

The server looked back and forth at the two men as he spoke, then continued, "And with some of the cuts, we offer seconds, of course. Would you like something from the bar?"

After both diners put in their drink order, Davis, eyes wide, leaned forward and asked Joel, "Seconds? You mean you can get *seconds* on prime rib here?"

Joel grinned at his colleague's mix of anticipation and incredulity. "Actually, yes. If you have room for seconds, they'll give you a smaller portion.

"Of what, just the prime rib?"

"Actually, of everything if you want," answered Joel. "More meat, more potatoes, more creamed spinach."

He grinned at Davis's flabbergasted expression. "Isn't that great?"

Davis shook his head in disbelief. "That's amazing. But I have a feeling one dinner will be plenty for me." He laughed. "Eating with you this trip, I'm really gonna to have to work out when I get home!"

Their drinks arrived, the waiter took their orders, then left. Joel offered a toast. "Cheers. To good health and good business."

"I'll drink to that," agreed Davis.

Joel paused for a moment, sipping his drink in thought. "You know, something just occurred to me. Maybe I've been afraid of a staff member leaving me, *not* because I don't want to have to go through finding a replacement.

"Maybe it's because I don't have a good handle on creating a simple strategy that you've been talking about in the S of SMILE."

Davis listened intently, cornbread sticks forgotten for the moment. "I don't follow you."

Joel leaned forward, convinced that he was onto something. "Look, I don't even have a simple strategy in mind that's easy to remember. I've just been thinking a mass of desperate thoughts about how we need to grow revenues, reduce our expenses, and get more out of our staff.

"So I'm thinking, if I lose someone, I'm going to have to get someone else to do what I'm not sure how to do, what I don't have the answers for." Joel was really warming up now, as words tumbled out more rapidly.

"That's it! I didn't have any answers, I wasn't sure what to do, so if I lose this person who has been with me for so many years, I'm going to have to start all over with someone new. And that's scary."

Joel gestured emphatically in the air as he continued.

"But what I now realize is, if I had a strategy that was simple enough for me to understand, I'd know that it's about executing the strategy, not just about doing things. And I wouldn't be afraid of losing people any longer." He sat back triumphantly.

Davis looked totally lost. "Uh, I'm still not following you, Joel."

"Don't you see?" Joel exclaimed excitedly. "I don't have a strategy like you do."

That's not a good thing, Davis thought, why are you so excited?

Joel continued his rant. "But if I did, I'd know what needs to get done. And I'd know that the key is finding the right people to get it done.

"It becomes all about the strategy driving me to find the right team, not just hoping whoever's on the team does their job. And being scared about 'starting over' if a staff member leaves."

Joel took a big swig from his drink. He grinned and said triumphantly, "I think I had an epiphany just now."

"Well, or something." Davis laughed his hearty laugh. "That was quite a speech!"

"It's almost like I don't have to be scared anymore," declared Joel. "Or at least, not scared of that. I just need to be able to put together and verbalize my strategy for my practice."

"Right, and because it'll be simple enough, you communicate it to your office team, and see who gets it, and who doesn't," Davis concurred.

"Or, if some don't get it, I see who wants to make the effort to get it," finished Joel. "Got it."

As the waiter returned, rolling a cart tableside, Joel looked across at Davis and remarked, "I can't believe it took me this long to realize this."

Then he thought for a moment. "Well, it took me this long to hear about your SMILE concept. So what took you so long to attend one of these conferences?" Joel laughed.

The men turned their attention to the waiter, who said, "Gentlemen, your spinning salad."

In a large bowl of ice sat a smaller metal bowl with salad greens in it. With his right hand, the server picked up a steel gravy boat containing salad dressing. He grasped the edge of the metal salad bowl with his left hand, and gave it a quick spin.

The mound of salad greens rotated quickly as the bottom of the bowl spun smoothly over the bed of ice, almost as if it were on ball bearings. As the bowl rotated, the waiter poured the dressing into the salad, raising his arm up and down as he poured.

The diners looked into the bowl of greens and saw the stream of dressing quickly creating what looked like one of those spinning spiral patterns used to hypnotize people on TV.

Davis looked at Joel. "Now there's a show!"

Joel nodded. "Not only that, the salad's good too."

The waiter finished tossing the salad, then divided it evenly between two frosty cold plates. After putting one in front of each man, he wheeled the cart away.

Picking another slice of bread from the basket, Joel returned to the topic at hand. "Okay, so I think I diverged and had that epiphany about needing a strategy. Let's get back to the M in SMILE. What do you keep in mind about this letter?"

Davis had already started wolfing down some of his salad. He took a moment to finish as his jaws worked overtime.

Joel noticed yet another look of contentment on Davis's face. "How's the salad, by the way?"

"Great." Davis showed two thumbs up. "To answer your question – for me, the main thing is remembering that I can't necessarily manage everyone the same way, because not everyone is the same type of person."

"That's pretty obvious, isn't it?" Joel took another bite of his own salad.

"You'd think so, but I think most of us tend to forget after a while. I certainly did. I'd be thinking, why doesn't Sally anticipate what I want her to do like Karen always does?

"And in reality, Karen and Sally are different people, of course. Karen is more intuitive, and Sally wants more direction so she feels she won't mess up and do the wrong thing."

"I see." Joel nodded and took another sip of his cocktail. "So while Karen probably wouldn't like you micromanaging her, maybe Sally wouldn't mind?"

"Right," confirmed Davis. "You have to remember that when someone takes initiative, they also take on some risk, the risk of that person not doing the right thing, or making a mistake. So when Karen takes initiative to do something that she figures should be done, she runs the risk that I didn't want that done."

Davis took another forkful of his salad. In spite of the food in his mouth, he managed to say, "But Sally doesn't want to take that risk. She'd rather I tell her what I want done, so she might ask me."

"Wouldn't that drive you crazy, if Sally's going to come to you to ask about every little thing?" Joel was puzzled.

"I'm just giving you an example. Sally might not come to me for every little thing, but she's the type who will want some confirmation of what I have in mind. So I have to manage Sally and Karen differently, and work with them in different ways."

"Got it." Joel's brow cleared. "But you were saying that you didn't always approach it this way?"

"No," said Davis, shaking his head. He picked up his cocktail, downed the last of his drink, and peered into the empty glass for a moment. "In the early days I sat there wondering why Sally was not more like Karen. But I came to realize that she can't be, and I'm the one who has to change and treat them like two different people.

"Sometimes I think, as dentists, and as busy as we are focusing on the technical aspects of our work, we try to find easier ways to do other things. So we hope that we can treat everyone exactly the same way because we think that's the fair and equitable thing to do."

Davis finished his salad and laid his fork down. "That happens to also be the easier thing to do, treating everyone exactly the same way. It takes less thought."

Joel took in every word as he sat back in his chair. "It might take less thought, but it's not the right thing to do."

"Correct."

Joel's distracted gaze went in the direction of a nearby chandelier overhead. He said, "In my case, I think I'm guilty of your earlier behavior too. I've caught myself sometimes thinking 'why can't Person A be more like Person B' or 'oh no, I'm going to have to handle Person C differently because she doesn't know about this thing'."

Turning back to Davis, Joel continued, "And I admit, I've even had thoughts of 'why do I have to spend so much time managing these folks, when they should just know to do their jobs?' You're saying with the M in your SMILE concept, that's the way it is. Manage."

Joel looked at Davis with an expression that implied a question.

"That's right, manage." Davis took his napkin and refolded it before returning it to his lap. "It's part of the job, part of owning a business with employees."

Just then the server reappeared. "Gentlemen, may I take your salad plates?" Telling them that dinner would arrive soon, he disappeared again, but not before Joel ordered a bottle of red wine.

Joel leaned back in his chair again and steepled his fingers. "So what do you do to 'manage' your office staff? Do you have things you keep in mind on this too?"

"I do." Davis took a corner of his napkin and absent-mindedly dabbed at the edge of the table. "The first thing I started with was to define the roles and duties of the individuals on my office team. Who does what, when, and how."

"That probably evolved over time, didn't it?" Joel un-steepled his fingers and crossed his arms across his chest.

"It did, but after a while, I actually created a summary of each role that I can print out – sort of like a job description you'd find in a larger company." Davis did a double-take as a chef walked by pushing another shiny domed cart of roasts. Then he leaned forward again.

"So these job descriptions came in handy whenever I hired someone new, but were also useful when I gave them to the folks who had already been working for me. That was a way of validating that we were on the same page regarding what I expected them to do."

Davis pushed his chair back slightly and crossed his legs. "You know, a lot of small businesses like ours don't bother with job descriptions, because they don't think they're necessary. I came to believe that they are essential, so I took the time to write them."

Joel was intrigued. "I can see how they would be great to give to someone who is just starting with you.

But how exactly did you handle it with your existing staff? You handed them a sheet of paper and said, 'Here, this is your job, read about it.'?"

The waiter returned to the table with the bottle of red wine Joel had ordered. After the pouring ceremony was complete, Davis answered Joel's last question.

"That's more or less what I did. You see, we have a very short morning meeting – five to ten minutes – every day to go over things. It's just to get set for what we need to keep our eyes on that day, the next day, and maybe what we should keep in mind if something out of the ordinary happened the previous day."

He took a sip from his wine glass and nodded appreciatively. "Nice choice of wine, Joel. I like it."

"Glad you do." Joel sipped his as well. "So it was during one of those morning meetings when you passed the job descriptions out for the first time?"

Davis leaned back and pondered the ceiling for a moment. "Actually, I think I waited until one of our monthly 'workshop' meetings to do that."

He looked at Joel and answered the question written on the man's face. "We have a monthly, two-hour meeting that I call 'workshop' time. It could be for continuing education, it could be to bring in a speaker, or it could be to discuss something internal at greater length.

"It was during one of those workshop sessions that I held the discussion about everyone's roles and job descriptions." Davis looked around the room, eyes seeking the prime rib cart that could contain their dinners.

"How did they react to the discussion?" Joel caught sight of a chef pushing a cart through the entrance to their dining room.

"Sort of what you'd expect. They'd all been working for me right along, of course, so when I passed out the job descriptions, there was silence. Almost like a question running through their minds like 'What's this?'."

Davis saw the cart too. "Is that for us?" he asked eagerly.

Joel laughed. "Well, not the whole cart, but I see our waiter over there talking to the chef."

The men both turned to watch the chef, as he cut slices of prime rib off one of the roasts standing on end. He finished plating up the dinners by adding the potatoes and creamed spinach. From a pot on the cart, au jus gravy was ladled right onto the cuts of meat.

The waiter returned to their table holding two dinner plates. Placing them in front of each diner, the waiter said, "I'll be right back with your Yorkshire pudding."

Davis looked at Joel. "What kind of pudding?"

"It's more like a popover, or a light bread," explained Joel. "It's one of the classic accompaniments of the dinner, the way they serve it here."

"Well it sure looks good," said Davis, as he grabbed his knife and fork.

"Bon appetit." Joel started to dig in as well. "So after your staff got over the surprise of reading about their jobs, were there any problems?"

"Not really." Davis had just tasted a piece of his prime rib. He closed his eyes and leaned back. "This … is incredible. It almost melts in my mouth!"

He opened his eyes and leaned forward again, knife and fork at the ready. "The descriptions were pretty much what they were already doing anyway. Remember, I wrote them. But I put it in the context of just wanting to be sure that we all agreed on what they were supposed to be doing."

Joel nodded as he savored a bite of meat.

"But here's an interesting twist that I don't think many owners of small businesses like ours do," said Davis. "I also had everyone become familiar with everyone else's job descriptions. So they would know what everyone else does."

"Why did you do that?" Joel stopped a forkful of creamed spinach on its way to his mouth.

Davis took another bite of prime rib and shrugged. "It was so each team member could see how she fit into the overall running of the office. So they could see how what they did related to the big picture."

He started to cut another piece of meat, then stopped. "And also to be able to help out if someone is out sick or just out of the office."

Joel let the forkful of spinach finish its journey, as he thought for a moment. "I can see that, but have you run into any problems with anyone refusing to help out, because they say 'it's not my job'?"

"Good question." Davis pointed his knife in Joel's direction. "I have once or twice, but not because of the job descriptions. When I run into that problem, I then know it's probably because I don't have the right person on the job."

He took his fork and scooped up a pile of mashed potatoes. "That kind of comment is usually from someone who is not a team player, in which case she's probably not the right person for my office team." The pile on the fork disappeared into his mouth.

At that moment, their server walked by.

"How is everything, gentlemen? Can I get you anything?

Davis looked up hopefully. "Any way we can get a couple more of those cornbread sticks?"

"Absolutely. I'll be right back."

Davis winked at Joel. "This is awesome. Thanks for bringing me here."

He suddenly remembered something. "By the way Joel, tonight's dinner is on me. No arguments. Besides, you picked up last night's."

Joel laughed. "Okay, you win. Thank you."

The server returned and placed a small basket on the table. Davis pulled back the napkin and withdrew a cornbread stick.

Joel picked up where they left off. "It sounds like you discovered that the job descriptions not only let you be sure you and your staff agreed on what they should be doing, but also let you see if you hired the right person to work for you."

"Right." Davis nodded, as he continued to eat.

"But do you run into any issues at all with people just sticking to their job descriptions, and not being willing to help out?"

Davis shook his head as he carefully put down his fork. "Not really. Not if I have the right people on board. Remember, it's still a small office, so everyone tries to pitch in and help when needed. I think our daily 10-minute meetings help reinforce that feeling."

He seized his fork again and eyed the next potential target on his plate. "That's also why I instituted team bonuses a couple of years ago."

"What's involved with that?" Joel reached over for the wine bottle and refilled Davis's glass before tending to his own.

"Thanks." Davis made a toasting motion with his glass and drank some. "The team bonuses are based on overall office performance targets. I have two levels for them to earn bonuses at."

"Two levels?"

"Two levels. You have to achieve the first level, before you can earn the second level. In my case, the first level is a revenue goal. The office must achieve that revenue goal and earn that level's bonus, before they are eligible to earn the second level bonus."

"What period of time does the revenue goal cover?" Joel stopped eating for the moment to concentrate on Davis's words.

"The goal is for each quarter. But every month I give the team updates on where we stand, how we're tracking to that goal." For his part, Davis continued to enjoy his meal with gusto.

"At the end of the quarter – actually about halfway into the month after the quarter, when I have final numbers – I tell my people if we've made the revenue goal for that period. If we did, then we look at the other metrics that determine the second-level bonus."

Joel picked up his wine glass. "And what's in the second-level bonus?"

"Really anything else you want to incentivize, depending on what you provide through your practice. It could be the number of implants you performed, or the number of clients who decided on laser therapy, or maybe you want to minimize the number of cancellations, so you set that as a target."

Davis's plate was now empty. He laid his fork and knife down, picked up his wine glass and looked over at Joel.

"After you've met the revenue targets for the quarter, then everyone's eligible for the second-level bonus. If they meet the targets you set for that level, they get the second bonus."

Davis took a longer sip of wine. "The bonuses by the way, are split equally among everyone on the office team. But if we don't meet the revenue target, then no bonus is paid out at all, even if we achieved the second-level metrics. Simple as that."

"Hmm." Joel absorbed what he heard, and nodded slowly. "I see. So each quarter you wipe the slate clean?"

"Yes. Each quarter has its own targets."

"How much of a bonus are you talking about?" asked Joel.

Davis finished his wine and set his glass down. "Well, that depends on what you think works. What I offer to my team might not work for you. It might be too low to make a difference for you, or too high for you to afford. But it's got to be high enough for them to want to work for it, and the right level for you to afford paying it."

He wiped his lips with his napkin. "See what I mean? Any bonus plan you put together has to have you making more money after you pay the bonus, compared to if you didn't. There's no point offering a bonus plan if you're left with less money in your pocket."

Joel's eyebrows were again knitted into a frown. "I'm not sure I'm following you there."

Davis looked straight up at the ceiling and thought for a moment. "Let me rephrase that. A bonus plan should incentivize people to perform better than they ordinarily would if they didn't have a bonus plan. The targets to earn the bonus should represent stretch targets, performance over and above what they've been achieving so far with no bonus incentive.

"So if they achieve stretch targets, you should be making more money, and that extra margin is what you're paying the bonus out of."

Davis drew imaginary lines on the table with his forefinger as he spoke, tracing the boundaries of ordinary versus stretch targets.

"Look at it this way. If they don't hit the stretch targets, you don't pay bonuses because they're at a level of production you expect of them for their regular pay.

"You have to be careful about that when you put together an incentive program. If you don't set the targets right, and you don't carefully check your math, all you end up doing is paying your team a bonus for doing what they should have done anyway. Then you're making less money."

He sat back, palms raised upward. "Does that make sense?"

Joel's expression had cleared. He nodded firmly. "Absolutely. I get it."

Once again, the waiter appeared to materialize out of nowhere. His entrance wasn't noticed because the dentists were so engrossed in their conversation.

"Would anyone care for seconds?"

Davis looked at Joel as if he were joshing. "What do you think? Are you going for it?"

"Not me." Joel patted his stomach. "But you go ahead, I'll watch."

Davis hesitated, seemingly undecided, then looked up at the server and said, "I think I'm going to have to pass." He almost sounded disappointed.

With coffee (yes) and dessert (no) orders squared away, the men resumed their discussion.

"I get that the first level bonus applies to revenue targets. Do you set one overall target, or do you divide it up into smaller pieces?" Joel asked.

"You can do what you want," Davis replied, "as long as it's not too complicated. I set targets for those of us who produce revenue – myself and my hygienists."

Joel nodded. "Makes sense. About the second level? Can you say more about what kinds of things would I include there?"

"Anything else you want to incentivize." Davis stopped as another server walked by with a plate of seconds for another diner. His eyes followed the plate all the way to a table across the room where the server set it down.

He turned back to Joel. "I create a target for things I want my office team to pay attention to during the quarter. If you, for example, want to get more folks to get implants, you put in a target for that. Or, if you're trying to cut down on the number of cancellations, you use that as a target."

The waiter arrived with their coffees, got them set up, and left.

"Just remember that whatever you incentivize, you've got to give them some direction on how to achieve the goal," said Davis, as he stirred some sweetener into his coffee.

"What kind of direction?" Joel poured some cream into his cup.

"I mean that you not only tell them the target, like 'reduce cancellations by 20% this quarter', but also be able to tell them things they can do to reduce cancellations." Davis took his turn with the cream.

Joel thought for a moment, holding his coffee cup with two hands. "So this is part of the 'Manage' in SMILE – where I manage my staff so they understand what they need to do."

"Exactly."

Joel fell silent and again pondered one of the ornate overhead light fixtures. Davis waited and sipped his coffee slowly.

Finally, Joel lowered his eyes, meeting Davis's steady gaze. "I think I'm getting it. Do you find that your daily meetings are the best way that you can manage your folks?"

"The daily meetings are short. They're primarily for addressing things that are happening that day, the day before, or what to keep in mind for the next day." Davis put his cup back on its saucer and continued.

"The monthly two-hour meeting is where I go more in depth about incentives and how to achieve them. That's not to say you couldn't give them a quick reminder during some of the daily meetings, of course."

Joel emptied his coffee cup with a final swig, and placed it back in its saucer. "You know, this has all been very interesting. And very helpful, of course." He pushed his chair back slightly and crossed his legs.

"I have to admit," he went on, "I'd been struggling with finding that middle ground between one extreme of having to tell my staff every single thing they should be doing, and the other extreme of expecting them to know what to do without being told."

Joel shifted in his chair and leaned forward. "Thanks to you, I now know I can set the agenda and use a longer meeting once a month to reinforce what we should be accomplishing, but have short daily meetings where I can remind them about things."

He sat back again and looked at Davis. "Did I get that right?"

Davis nodded. "That sounds about right. The meeting length and frequency has to fit your needs, but I wouldn't go less frequently than once a month for those longer 'workshop' meetings."

The waiter showed up again. "Will there be anything else, gentlemen?"

Davis looked at Joel. "Anything?" Joel shook his head.

"I'll take the check, please," said Davis as he reached for his wallet.

Summary – "M" = Manage

To manage your office team and hold them accountable to the objectives you've established, have the right incentives and communication structure in place.

• Establish two types of meetings, daily and monthly.

• Determine agenda and content for these meetings that make them useful for you and your team. Do not hold meetings just to meet.

• Consider offering compensation incentives for your people to strive for, including revenue and non-revenue targets.

• Create job descriptions for all team members, and have them learn about each other's jobs.

• Hold team members accountable to the jobs you're paying them to do. If they're not doing what they committed to, guide them, remediate them, or part ways with them.

Remember to manage to your strategic objectives, and ensure that your team members are performing to achieve those objectives.

"I" = Initiative

"Folks who never do any more than they get paid for,
never get paid for any more than they do."
--Elbert Hubbard

The next morning's conference sessions at the Marriott proved more productive for Joel than the previous couple of days. That was in part because he attended breakouts that were on topics particularly interesting to him, like the one on hygiene time management, something he could discuss with his hygienists.

His energy level was also up because the SMILE discussion with Davis was resonating well with him.

He felt more settled about how Davis's SMILE could help with his struggles with his office staff. Or rather, as Joel made his way down the crowded corridor toward "Conference Central", he had some ideas of what he would change, to better work with his people.

The suggestion about everyone getting to know everyone else's job was a good one. He had always assumed that everyone knew, because they all worked together in a small office. In reality, each staff member only generally knew what the others did, but not much about the details.

They probably didn't much care, either, Joel mused as he strode toward the crowd of people clustered around the notice boards. But after he returned home from this conference, he would have to make sure they cared.

Engrossed in thought, Joel looked straight ahead without seeing. His eyes suddenly focused and he found himself face to face with Davis.

"Whoa!" If Davis hadn't put his hand out to meet Joel's jacket lapel, the Denver dentist would have run smack into him. "What's the rush?"

"Oh, hey Davis!" Joel grinned sheepishly. "Sorry about that, I was lost in my own world."

"No kidding." Davis dropped his arm, when he saw that it was safe to do so. He looked around as if he didn't want anyone else to hear him. "Say, what are your plans this afternoon? Any sessions that you feel you can't miss?"

Joel opened his conference agenda. "No, actually I was thinking that I might hang out at my hotel this afternoon, and catch up on some other things."

He closed the booklet. "Why do you ask?"

"Well, how about we grab lunch somewhere away from here?" Davis waved in the direction of the ballroom where the conference lunches had been held. "I wouldn't mind a break from the standard conference menu for a change."

He looked over Joel's shoulder and out the large window looming behind. "I also wouldn't mind hearing your next pick for a good lunch place." He gave Joel a friendly clap on the left arm as he spoke.

"Sounds good." Joel looked at his watch. "I've got one more session before the lunch hour. I'll meet you by the shuttle stop outside the hotel, and we'll ride back to the Wharf."

* * * * * *

It was just after 12:15. Joel dumped his conference bag onto his bed. Housekeeping had already cleaned his room, so he hung his Do Not Disturb sign on the doorknob facing the hallway.

As he fished out his phone, he decided to make a quick call to his wife.

"Hi dear, how's it going?" Lora answered, in the car, headed to the office.

"Really good. I'm about to head out to lunch with Davis." Joel shrugged out of his sport coat while he spoke, and wiggled into his windbreaker. "We're both skipping the conference sessions this afternoon, so I figured I'd take him to another San Francisco eating landmark."

The phone slipped out and fell to the carpet. He retrieved it from the floor, brought it back up to his ear and said, "Sorry, I dropped the phone. Are you headed to the office?"

"Yes, I am. I was going to pick up those folders you asked me to bring home." Lora made a right turn at the light.

"Thanks, dear."

Lora pulled into their office's parking lot and parked. "Are you going to have another chat with Davis about his SMILE?" She grinned at the pun she intended.

"Definitely." Joel nodded, 950 miles away in the City by the Bay. "It's all starting to make sense, and I can't wait to finish the conversation."

Husband and wife said their goodbyes, and Joel tapped the End button on his phone.

During the shuttle ride back from the Marriott to the Fisherman's Wharf area, the dentists had decided to meet in the lobby of Joel's hotel. He pulled his door shut, pushed on it briefly to be sure it was latched, and headed down the hallway.

Davis had his back to the lobby as he surveyed the traffic on the street outside passing by the window. Joel approached from behind and tapped him on the back.

"Ready?"

Turning, Davis asked, "What's today's culinary destination?" He grinned broadly.

Joel looked at his watch. "Seeing that it's 12:45, why don't we go to the Buena Vista Café for lunch? It's not far."

"Is that where they invented Irish Coffee?" Davis sounded eager at the prospect of going.

Joel laughed. "Well, I think they claim to have been first in the U.S. to re-create the original that was served in Ireland. Apparently Buena Vista Cafe serves two *thousand* of those every day!"

"I'm in. Let's go." Davis motioned with his right arm and started walking to the door.

Joel fell in step with the other dentist as they passed the threshold and continued outside onto the sidewalk along Beach Street. Suddenly Davis stopped.

"Wait, I don't know which way."

Joel continued walking. "Keep going. It's just up a block or so at Hyde."

Davis scooted to catch up with Joel and matched his stride. "You sure know your way around."

"Old haunts from past conference trips." Joel shrugged. He glanced to the right as they crossed Leavenworth, the blue of the water sparkling through and beyond the pier struts at the end of the street. "I do like it here, though."

"Well, are you ready for the next letter?" asked Davis in a mock dramatic tone. "What is it, and what do you think it's about?"

"I," replied Joel, "for Initiative." He looked quickly over his left shoulder, and said "Cross here."

The two men crossed Beach Street to the sidewalk on the other side.

Without breaking stride, Joel continued, "And I'm going to guess that Initiative probably has to do with your office staff taking the initiative to do the right things?"

"That's pretty much it." Davis nodded.

"Then I know I'm going to be asking you again about how you reach that balance between them taking initiative and you having to tell them what to do." The men had almost reached the entrance to the café, at the corner across from where they were waiting for the light to change.

"It definitely is related to the previous part, the M in SMILE," explained Davis. The light changed and they started to cross the street, carefully stepping over the tracks embedded in the pavement for the San Francisco cable car system.

Joel pointed to the left, up the hill. At the crest of the hill stood a cable car with its timeless silhouette, framed sharply against the blue of the clear sky above. "There's a photo op for you, Davis."

Davis looked, struck by the view, before the rumble of the cable underneath the tracks reminded him that he stood right in the middle of Hyde Street. He hurried to the other side, where Joel waited for him under the neon sign that jutted out from the corner of the building. They entered the café.

"There's an empty table over there." Joel started toward it. The two men took seats facing the window looking out toward Alcatraz.

"When it gets crowded, sometimes people will just come up to your table and ask if you would mind if they join you," said Joel, indicating the two other empty chairs at their table. "If that happens, we might have to agree, out of politeness."

Davis looked around at the other mostly empty seats in the café, including a number of open stools at the bar. "For now anyway, it looks like there are plenty of seats open." He grinned. "Maybe they knew two dentists would be in the house!"

A server came up to their table. "Hi, welcome to the Buena Vista Café!" she said cheerfully. "Can I get you something to drink?"

After the men asked for Irish coffees and menus, the server left them to resume their conversation.

"You were saying that the I is related to the M in SMILE?" asked Joel. He unfolded a napkin and placed it on his lap.

"It is." Davis looked out the window at the view, taking it all in. "Even though you have a handle on how to manage your team – the M – you still must have the right people on your team. The right people with the I – the initiative – to do what's right for your business."

He reached for the menu lying on the table and opened it. "What's good here?"

Joel opened his copy and skimmed the page. "Being this close to the Wharf, they have a variety of Dungeness crab options. You can get it fresh, half or whole, as crab cakes, on an English muffin as a melt, on a salad, or even in an omelet – they serve breakfast all day."

He looked at Davis and grinned. "Enough of a choice for you? That is, if Dungeness crab is something you're still interested in."

"Are you kidding?" Davis retorted. "Of course I'm interested." He went back to studying the menu.

The server came back with their Irish coffees and placed them on the table. "Are you ready to order?"

The dentists placed their orders and the waitress collected their menus and returned to the kitchen. Joel raised his glass mug in a toast.

"To good health, good friendships, and the I in SMILE."

Davis acknowledged with his mug. "I'll drink to that." He took a sip and smacked his lips. "That's really good."

Licking the cream off the edge of his coffee mug, Joel resumed the discussion.

"So you were saying that you need the right person with the right amount of initiative. How do you know if someone has it?"

Davis gave it a moment's thought, as he took another sip of his drink. "I guess you don't at first, but you have to create an environment where you can test it out."

"I've been burned in the past," said Joel, "where a staff member has told me that I can rely on her to take care of something, and in the end she doesn't do a good job of it." He started to feel irritated again as memories surfaced.

"Did you supervise her – or at least track what was going on – when you first gave her the responsibility?"

Joel shook his head, his lips now compressed into a thin line. "Not really. She said she could handle it, and seemed a little miffed if I was going to look over her shoulder. It was almost like she was thinking I didn't trust her."

Davis leaned forward and peered at Joel. "So you didn't insist on keeping tabs on her early in the process?"

"Well, I didn't want to offend her," Joel replied, sounding defensive. "She kept telling me she would handle it."

It was Davis's turn to shake his head. "You can't let one of your employees push you off like that. You're the one who's paying her, so you have a right to know that she's going to do the job right."

Joel took another sip of his drink. Just then their server returned to the table, holding two plates.

"Dungeness crab omelet with the sourdough toast?"

Davis pointed right in front of him, as she set his plate down.

"And the Dungeness crab Cobb salad," she announced as she put the other plate in front of Joel. "Anything else right now, ketchup or Tabasco?"

"No, thank you," said Joel.

Davis had already reached for his sourdough toast, and was eyeing it closely. "San Francisco sourdough, huh?" He took a bite and closed his eyes.

Joel looked up from prepping his salad, his grouchy mood broken momentarily by mild amusement. The dentist from Long Island could even get enthused about toast.

Davis opened his eyes. "Why can't I ever get this kind of bread back at home?"

"You can. All you have to do is go to the Boudin Bakery website and order some." Joel grinned as he dipped a forkful of crab into the dressing.

"Very funny." The other man started in on his omelet.

For a few moments the diners concentrated on their food, checking out the view beyond the windows. The plaza teemed with people crisscrossing the sidewalks and street between. Inside the café a few more customers had arrived, but there were still plenty of open seats.

After he broke a slice of toast in two, Davis returned to what they were discussing before their food arrived.

"Like I said before, if you give someone the responsibility for doing something, you have to be sure they're going to do it right. And in order to be sure they're doing it right, you have to look at what they do."

Joel stopped his fork in mid-air, on its way to his mouth. "How do I do that without offending the person? I supposedly hired them for their experience. I don't want to treat them like they have no experience."

His fork finished its trajectory to his mouth. With a bulging cheek, he complained, "Besides, if they have the experience, I shouldn't have to spend all my time managing them."

"That's not the point." Davis waved his fork impatiently. "There's plenty of middle ground between turning someone loose and keeping constant tabs on them."

He used the side of his fork to cut another piece from his omelet. Devouring the bite, he sat back and folded his arms.

Joel grinned again despite his mood. "Enjoying yourself?"

Davis nodded, savoring the taste of his lunch. He swallowed. "Definitely."

He circled back to their discussion topic. "Back on what we were saying, it's like any other matter of trust. You give the new team member things to do, or maybe a project, and see how they do."

Davis reached for his Irish coffee and took a sip. "I like to think of it as building incremental levels of trust, one step at a time."

He held up his hand suddenly. "And by the way, I don't mean give them a project or something on your critical path."

"Critical path?" Joel asked, words muffled by a mouthful of salad.

"Yes. Something that if it's not done right, would mess you up for some time or take a bunch of your time to fix." Davis waved his hands for emphasis.

"That's how you gain trust in how they work," he went on, reaching for his fork again. "By seeing how they do with non-critical tasks in the office."

"But that's not always possible," protested Joel. He used his napkin on his lips. "If I get a new office manager, for example, I have to have her work on what she would be responsible for."

He threw his napkin back in his lap. "I can't have her working on busy work while I decide if she can cut it or not," he complained.

Davis shrugged. "In that case, you have her do what she's supposed to do, but you take the time to supervise or double-check that she's doing it properly."

He raised both his hands, palms down, in a "slow-down" gesture to Joel. "Don't forget what we're talking about here. We're talking about finding the right people who have the right level of initiative to work in your practice."

Davis reached for his water, took a gulp, and finished his thought. "To see what kind of initiative they have, you give some direction – some clues – about what you want them to do, and see if they have the initiative to do it without being guided every step of the way."

Joel looked silently out the window as he digested Davis's comments.

"Are you still there?" Davis knocked on the table with his knuckles.

Frustration furrowed in his brow, Joel turned to Davis. "Yes, I am. It's just that this has been the most frustrating part of the past several years. I've got people who don't seem to give much of a hoot any more. And one or two who have the nerve to say that I'm not much fun to be around."

He turned back to the window again, blinking rapidly, mouth set in a grim thin line. "The gall of some of them to even think that, when they're the ones who should be shaping up!"

Davis waited a moment for the other man's emotions to settle. He said gently, "You can fix this. We talked about this before. If you get the M in SMILE set up right, that'll help you with your I."

As Joel turned to look at him again, Davis continued, "You get the right objectives set up in your S component, and they'll have guidance for their behaviors. Reinforce it with your regular staff meetings, so they'll remember how they're supposed to behave. That's the job of the M. Then when you put that together with folks who have the right levels of initiative, they will want to do the right things to meet the objectives of your business."

Davis looked as if he suddenly just realized something. "So you see? That's how the M sets up the I in SMILE. If you've got goals that are simple enough, that everyone can understand, they have some guidance of what you expect from their daily behaviors. If you communicate those and reinforce them regularly, they'll remember."

He looked at Joel triumphantly and stabbed his forefinger in the air for emphasis. "And if you do those things well, you'll be able to clearly see who has initiative, and who doesn't. You won't have to wonder. You'll know when you need to replace someone."

Joel was slowly nodding as Davis spoke, frustration starting to dissipate. "I think I'm getting it." He returned his attention to his lunch, which had been sitting neglected for some time.

Davis picked up his fork again and attacked the remnants of his omelet. With his spoon to catch the last of the sauce, he finished cleaning his plate.

"So let's recap," proclaimed the dentist from Long Island, as he wiped the corners of his mouth with his napkin. "The I in SMILE is about finding the right people with the right levels of initiative. Folks you can count on to do what's needed without checking with you every time, or being told what to do every time. Okay?"

Joel nodded while checking his plate for any last morsels of Dungeness crab.

"And assuming you've got your M act together, and communicate it clearly to your team, you've got some guidelines that help you see who's got initiative, and who doesn't. Understood?"

Joel nodded again, lining up his knife and fork on his now empty plate.

"Armed with that, you give your people only just enough guidance, and double-check in the early going that they're doing the right things. With the right results. Roger?" Davis ticked the points off on his fingers as he spoke.

"Roger."

"Do you have any questions, Dr. Chenoski?" asked Davis with a smile.

"Nope." Joel shook his head. "Sorry if I was a little testy there," he apologized ruefully.

"No problem. I can certainly understand your feelings of frustration." Davis drained his coffee mug and set it back down.

"One thing that just occurred to me," said Joel. "If you start seeing signs that someone isn't working out, or may not work out, how long do you wait before you let them go?"

At that moment, their server reappeared at their table. "Well, I hope everything was good." She eyed their empty plates. "Sure looks like it was."

Joel looked at Davis and indicated their coffee mugs. "Got time for another round?"

Davis looked at his watch. "I'm good. I don't have to meet my wife until about 3:30 or 4:00."

The server collected their plates and said, "I'll be right back with your drinks."

Davis was struck with an idea. "Say, do you want to join us for dinner tonight? My wife and I were just going to find someplace quiet and low key."

"Oh no, I wouldn't want to spoil your evening," replied Joel. "I know you and your wife haven't really had dinner together yet, since I've monopolized your time the past two nights!"

"Not a problem. I'm sure Malita would love to meet you," offered Davis.

Joel shook his head. "Thanks again, but you two ought to have your quiet dinner together. Besides, I have to take care of some work I actually brought with me."

"What, you mean you have a couple of patients who traveled with you to San Francisco?" Davis laughed loudly.

Joel grinned, his grumpiness all but forgotten. "You know what I mean. Paperwork. Besides, I ought to catch up with my own wife. We really haven't had much chance to talk."

Their server returned with their drinks, and left the check. "No rush guys, I'll just leave this for whenever you're ready."

Joel took a sip of his coffee drink, and remembered his train of thought. "Oh yes, so I was about to ask you how long you wait before you let someone go, if you don't see signs of them working out?"

Davis lowered his mug, and nodded. "I actually give my office team members regular performance evaluations. A lot of people say these should be done annually, and from what I've read, even more of us dentists don't even do any evaluations at all."

"How often do you do yours?"

"If someone's just joined my practice, I'll do a 90-day evaluation, just to be sure we're both heading in the same direction," Davis explained. "It's not a real formal process. I'll write a short memo to her and outline the key things that look like they're going well, and some things where we both keep an eye on. Then we'll have a conversation about it."

He took another sip from his mug. "Then I'll do another evaluation six months from then, and every six months afterward.

"The interval is not important. The main thing is to have regular communications going on about how you think your team member is doing. It's also important for her to be able to tell you how it's going from her point of view too."

Joel nodded, acknowledging the other man's point. "That's how I'd have the chance to tell her where she's going off track and see if she takes the initiative to correct it, right?"

Davis pointed at Joel's chest. "Now you're talking. The team member has to have the feedback on what to correct, if she's going to be able to do anything about it."

He sat back and clasped his fingers together. "You can't wait to see if it gets any better, without giving the person feedback on what you want them to fix."

Both men drained their mugs, and settled the check. Joel stood up, indicated the table and said, "How was your lunch?"

"Fabulous." Davis patted his stomach. "Really hit the spot."

As they headed back out to the street, they heard faint sounds of a guitar playing and some singing.

In a small plaza across Beach Street from where they stood, a group of people gathered around a street entertainer.

"Hey, let's cross over here for a moment," said Joel. "I want to see if that's the guitar guy – it sure sounds like him."

"Guitar guy?" Davis hurried to catch up to Joel, who was already crossing the street.

"Yes, he's been here for ages, around Ghirardelli or the Wharf area," explained Joel. "The guy's great. He'll pick on someone walking by, then make up a song about that person, usually poking fun at them."

The two men approached the group focused on an older African-American man with a hat, wearing a sweater, his guitar case open on the sidewalk with dollar bills and change in it.

As the street entertainer finished a song with a flourish, the group broke out into laughter and applause. Davis and Joel edged up and stood unobtrusively toward the back – or so they thought.

Their arrival did not go unnoticed by the guitar player, who looked straight at Davis.

"Hello there, young man!" the guitarist called out. "And what brings you here?"

Davis looked around for a moment, then realized the entertainer was talking to him. "Uh, I'm just here in town for a conference."

The singer/guitarist laughed heartily. "What are you conferencing about?"

A little self-consciously, Davis gestured in the opposite direction. "I'm attending the American Dental Association conference."

Under his breath, Joel muttered to himself, "Uh-oh, too much information."

The guitar man jumped right on it. "So, are you a dentist?" Another hearty laugh.

Davis nodded. "Afraid so." Others in the spectator group chuckled.

"I *love* dentists!" exclaimed the guitar man, tipping his hat. "I dedicate this song to you!"

With that, he started strumming his guitar, and to the tune of a nondescript melody, he sang:

> *There once was a dentist named Keith*
>
> *For whom nothing was ever beneath.*
>
> *To one patient he said,*

With a great deal of dread...

"I think I lost four of your teeth!"

The guitar man laughed uproariously at his own melodic limerick, as did Joel and the other spectators. Davis, blushing, shook his head and smiled.

The dentists started to leave, and as they passed the guitar man, Davis dropped a bill into the guitar case.

"Thank you, my man! I hope you find the teeth!"

They could still hear his cackling laughs echoing as they crossed the street and headed back toward their hotels.

Davis grinned and looked at Joel. "Well, that was an experience."

"I forgot to warn you about giving him too much information," admitted Joel. "As you found out, he can use it against you."

The men started along Beach Street in the direction of Joel's hotel. In stride, Davis turned to Joel and said, "One last thing about Initiative that you ought to keep in mind."

"What's that?"

"We already agree that the right level of initiative has to do with your team member being able to do what she needs to do to get the job done. Right?"

Joel nodded.

"And she does what she needs to do without being told all the time, or without checking with you every time she makes a move."

"Right." Joel nodded again, eyes on the sidewalk as he walked and listened.

"Well," Davis went on, "also keep in mind that a person can show initiative by doing what's necessary to learn the right things, in order to do her job well. Again, without being told, or by asking for help from you."

Joel stopped abruptly and turned to Davis, who almost ran into him because of the unexpected move.

"That's a great point!" exclaimed Joel. "People who want to do a good job, are also usually folks who find out what knowledge and tools they require, to do a good job."

"Exactly." Davis smoothed out his jacket from the near-collision.

Joel resumed his walking, but at an even faster rate, eyes set on the distance, apparently intent on getting somewhere.

Davis did a quick jog to catch up, and fell in stride with him again. "What's the sudden rush?" he puffed.

"You've given me some great ideas, Davis." Joel continued his pace, eyes still straight ahead, no longer downcast at the pavement. "When I get back to my hotel, I'm going to start taking notes on the evaluations I'll be putting together for my staff."

He slowed as they reached the entrance to the Courtyard. "In fact, I'll be writing notes on everything we've talked about the past couple of days. I'm going to start getting my S together, figure out the meeting structure for my M, and think about the evaluations that will work for the I."

Davis thought for a moment about Joel's words. "Did you just say you're going to … get your S together?" Both men laughed uproariously as a passer-by gave them a quick look.

Joel, eyes glowing with energy, looked at Davis. "I have you to thank for helping me see all this," he said warmly, extending his hand.

Davis took the handshake, and said, "But we haven't finished with the L and the E yet!"

"I know," agreed Joel. "But this gives me a lot to get started with, and I now have a much clearer picture of the part that's been sorely lacking for me."

The automatic doors to the hotel opened as Joel approached. He stopped in the threshold and looked back at the other dentist with a grin.

"Are you still available tomorrow to finish out the spelling of SMILE?"

"Are you kidding me?" Davis smirked. "I can't wait to see which restaurant you've got in mind!"

Summary – "I" = Initiative

Be certain your team has initiative. Don't put up with people who only act if you tell them to.

• Build your trust in them incrementally with tasks or projects. You have the right to expect them to earn your trust.

• Give clues about what you want them to do, but don't give outright answers. Evaluate their initiative by seeing what answers they come up with.

• The M sets up the I in SMILE. If you give the right direction, people can develop guidelines about expected behavior, and apply their initiative.

• Have regular performance evaluations where you give feedback, and use those results to see if your team member has the right levels of initiative to be on your office team.

• Remember that initiative is also demonstrated by the person doing what's necessary to acquire the knowledge and skills to do the job well.

Initiative is a personality trait. Surround yourself with people who have initiative. Those lacking it, probably think working for you is "only a job."

"L" = Loyalty

"Do what you do so well that they will want to see it again and bring their friends."

--Walt Disney

It was the last full day of the conference, and Joel's restlessness showed, with thoughts and ideas bouncing off the walls of his mind. After his lunch with Davis yesterday, he had returned to his room to start working on what the S, the M, and the I in SMILE meant to him and his practice.

Joel made some pretty good progress, brainstorming about how he could craft objectives that would be simpler and easier to understand by his office staff. He thought about what he would need to do to establish regular staff meetings, and more importantly how he could make those meetings a lot more useful to them all.

Last night, he was so engrossed in his train of thought, he lost track of time when his cell phone rang. It was his wife.

"Where have you been?" exclaimed Lora good-naturedly. "I haven't heard from you in a while."

"Oh, sorry," apologized Joel. "I just got so wrapped up in what I was doing, I lost all track of time." He looked at his watch. "I even forgot all about dinner."

His wife asked what he was working on, so he proceeded to tell her about the discussion he and Davis had over lunch at the Buena Vista Café. He went on to tell Lora about the results of his brainstorms during the past few hours in his hotel room.

Back in the present, Joel recalled the rest of his conversation with his wife last night, remembering with a smile what she said to him just before they said their good-nights.

"Well, honey, you go get something to eat. It won't do much good to come up with a great plan, but not have any energy to put it into action!"

He ended up just ordering room service afterward, so he could eat and continue his thinking and making notes.

That's what made him antsy, what he accomplished in his hotel room last night, combined with what he anticipated from his meeting with Davis today.

The dentists had decided to meet over lunch again, as both men realized that all of the sessions they were each interested in were to take place in the morning.

Davis had planned to take the rest of the afternoon off to do some sightseeing with his wife. They were going to stay in town another couple of nights. Joel had booked a flight leaving SFO just before 6 o'clock that evening, arriving in Denver before 9:30. He'd be able to sleep in his own bed tonight.

The morning for Joel flew by, punctuated by a workshop on etchable ceramic restorations that he had been wanting to attend. Before he knew it, he was on the shuttle headed back to the Courtyard. When he got up to his room, he quickly gathered the rest of his things and finished packing his rolling carry-on. His briefcase strapped to the top end of his carry-on, Joel left the room, letting the door close behind him. He started down the hallway toward the elevator, bags in tow.

At the front desk, the hotel clerk greeted him. "Checking out?" she asked.

"Yes," replied Joel. "Can you also store my bags until I come back for the shuttle to the airport this afternoon?"

Check out now completed and bags stored away, Joel turned to scan the lobby. There sat Davis in an overstuffed chair, apparently captivated by yet another sightseeing brochure.

He looked up as Joel approached. "There you are. All set?" He gestured in the general direction of the front desk.

Joel nodded. "Yes. I'll be back for my bags when it's time to catch the shuttle to the airport."

"Are you sure you have enough time for lunch?" Davis stood up.

"Absolutely." Joel grinned. "I want to take you to a dim sum place in Chinatown! Are you up for it?"

Davis's eyes widened with anticipation. "That sounds like a treat! I don't often get the chance to have authentic Chinese food."

The two dentists went out onto the sidewalk in search of a cab. In just a couple of minutes, one pulled up and they piled in.

"New Asia Restaurant on Pacific Avenue, please," instructed Joel to the cab driver.

Without a word the driver started his meter and pulled away quickly from the curb.

Davis turned to Joel. "You really know your places, don't you," he said appreciatively.

Joel shrugged. "Like I said, I've been to a couple of these ADA meetings here before. My wife and I always enjoyed the time we had to explore after the conference was over."

The cab driver headed down Columbus Avenue, weaving through the busy noon-time traffic. Quiet for the moment, Joel looked out the window at the passing scenery.

They passed the same views he saw on the very first morning he rode the shuttle bus to the conference venue. The same morning he met Davis sitting next to him on the bus, just a short few days ago.

After a right turn onto Pacific Avenue, the taxi started up the hill. Davis peered through the windshield, where the street appeared to rise and meet the sky. He pointed straight ahead. "It almost looks like you can drive straight up and off the other side."

The vehicle pulled to a stop by the curb. Joel paid the driver and got out, with Davis close behind. The dentists stopped for a moment to examine the restaurant's unusual front entrance.

It looked as if a giant hole had been drilled through the stone wall of the restaurant about three feet above the sidewalk, with a semicircular awning that protruded from the top of the circle, capping the opening. A cutout with straight sides connected the bottom of the circle to the sidewalk, providing a short walkway to the front door, and completing the appearance of an enormous old-fashioned keyhole.

As soon as the men passed through the door, the building opened up before their eyes. Inside, the cavernous two-level dining room was brightly lit with large chandeliers hanging from the ceiling. Sparkling turrets protruded from the huge glass-walled mezzanine, revealing tables in the alcoves above.

Across the enormous first floor a sea of tables rippled with waves comprised of the heads of diners bobbing and turning as they ate, talking and laughing with each other. The two men were also hit with the incredible noise of the restaurant, a hundred conversations going on, clattering dishes, clanging pot covers. The cacophony was an almost tangible blanket of sounds thrown in their faces.

"How many, please?" shouted the greeter at the reception podium, trying to be heard above the din.

It wasn't until the dentists were seated at a table that Davis caught sight of the women pushing carts stacked with steaming hot food. They crisscrossed paths across the entire dining room, somehow covering every table without appearing to have an organized route.

Davis pointed. "Is that where we get lunch?" he half-shouted, jokingly.

"Actually, yes," explained Joel, voice raised above the din, "but they'll come by to see what we want." He poured tea from the metal teapot already on their table, into the short, stout ceramic teacups with no handles.

"Do you go for dim sum much when you're home on Long Island?" Joel took a sip of his tea.

Davis shook his head. "No, I don't. Actually I'm not that familiar with it. Is dim sum a specific type of food?"

"The literal translation of the Chinese term 'dim sum' is 'touch the heart'," explained Joel. "But think of them as hors d'oeuvres or small plates. That way you can try a bunch of different dishes."

Just then, a server arrived with her cart, steam wisping from multiple stacks of round tins containing the Chinese delicacies. It almost looked as if she had several shiny smokestacks rising from her cart. "What would you like, gentlemen?"

Joel jumped into action. "Do you have *shiu mai*, and *hah gow*? How about *don tut* and *cha-siu bow*?

Davis's head swiveled back and forth from the cart to the table, as he watched the server place several small tins and plates of food in front of them.

The server went on her way, and with his pair of chopsticks, Joel motioned to the food. "Dive in!"

Davis used his chopsticks, though less skillfully than Joel, to put some items on the small empty plate in front of him. He picked up one item and peered at it.

"What is this?" he asked politely.

"It's called *hah gow* in Cantonese," replied Joel, already chowing down. "It's a shrimp dumpling."

Davis took a tentative bite, and nodded his head. "Delicious. I've never had this before." He wolfed down the remaining half.

"I hate to get back to business," said Joel as he refilled Davis's tea cup, "but I'd like to cover the remaining SMILE letters before I board that plane tonight."

"Absolutely, that was the deal," said Davis, his response muffled by a full mouth. Joel looked up and saw that his dining companion's enthusiasm for the cuisine was quickly gaining momentum as he tried each item.

Davis swallowed and took a gulp of tea. "Let's talk about the L. What do you think that's about?"

Joel took a bite from a *shiu mai*, and had to pause before answering. "I know it stands for loyalty. Based on what we already talked about, I'll say … how to build your staff's loyalty to you and your business?"

"Right word, wrong application of it," countered Davis. He looked at the tin that Joel had just picked from. "What was that you just ate, by the way?"

"It's called *shiu mai*. Pork dumpling." He pushed the container closer to Davis. "What do you mean, wrong application?"

Davis selected a piece and put it on his plate, then put his chopsticks down. "It's not about building the staff's loyalty to the business. It's about building your clients' loyalty to your practice. And it's about getting your team to constantly do the things they should be doing to earn and build your clients' loyalty."

Joel sipped his tea thoughtfully, staring straight ahead without focus. He slowly nodded, as he cradled his cup between two hands.

"I see." He looked at Davis. "So that's what you meant, the first day we met, when you said you grew your business by really connecting with your existing patients."

The other man was about to say something when Joel cut him off.

"Clients! I mean clients!" Joel hastily corrected himself.

Davis shot him a nasty look, picked up his chopsticks again and pointed them at Joel. "Exactly right. We built a lot of loyalty with our clients. And loyal clients are more likely to keep their recare appointments, and also ask about other services.

"Not that we're trying to manipulate our clients, because we really do want the best for their dental care." He picked up what looked like a white ball of bread and inspected it. "What is this, anyway?"

Joel grinned. "Try it. That's called *cha-siu bow*. It's got Chinese style barbeque roast pork inside." He pointed. "But be sure to peel off the paper liner on the bottom first."

Davis took a huge bite as Joel went on. "So what are the things you do to create loyalty on the part of your clients?"

It took a moment before Davis could answer. "Again, it's a combination of having the team remember things that they should be doing every day, and reminding them of it during our morning meetings. Or, if it's a bigger topic, or a new one, I might use one of the longer monthly meetings for that."

He took another gulp of tea before continuing. "I personally think that the most important thing for any team member to remember is how much they can affect the impression a client gets of our business."

Joel refilled Davis's tea cup. "I agree with that. If, for example, my receptionist is in a bad mood and she acts that way in front of a ... client, it'll rub off." This time Joel remembered not to say 'patient'.

"Right." Davis popped the remainder of the *cha-siu bow* in his mouth. "And if that client was referred to you by one of your existing clients, he might go back to the guy who referred, and say 'I didn't think that dentist was all that good.' Then your original client might start re-thinking his impression of your practice."

Davis surveyed the table to see what he hadn't yet tried. He pointed at what looked like a mini-custard pie tart. "What's that?"

"*Don tut*," replied Joel. "It's like an egg custard tart. Good for a dessert." He picked up the menu from the table. "I'm going to order some Chinese noodles, are you interested?"

"I'll eat whatever you order. With you as my culinary guide these past few days, I'll always put myself in your hands." Davis saluted in mock respect.

Joel laughed and signaled a passing waiter, one of the few not pushing a steam cart.

Turning back to Davis, he asked, "Do you know what percentage of your new clients are referrals, versus someone who saw your ads or your listing?"

Davis nodded. "I'd say almost three-fourths of our new clients were referred by one of our existing clients. I appreciate that fact, and I'm going to do everything in my power to make sure that we create the kind of loyalty with the new client that our existing one has."

He reached for another *cha-siu bow* and peeled the bottom paper off it. Davis waved it around as he continued, "See, that's the ultimate demonstration of loyalty. If a client thinks so much of our service and the experience of coming in that he'll tell someone else to come see us too, I'm flattered."

He took a big bite of the *cha-siu bow*, almost devouring it whole. After he swallowed, he pointed out a common fact.

"You know how it is, Joel. People don't exactly like or look forward to going to the dentist. We wish it were different, but that's how human nature works for most people."

Joel nodded. "Yeah, if only it were, 'I can't wait to get to the dentist again!' So I see your point. That someone would refer is the highest compliment." He reached out with his chopsticks to take the remaining *shiu mai* from the metal basket, then stopped, food in mid-air.

"But what are those things you have your front office say or do? How do you keep the front office thinking about client loyalty?"

Davis dabbed at the corners of his mouth with his napkin. "Okay, time out. Remember that my 'front office' is a location in my office suite. It doesn't do, talk, or think."

He sat back with the hint of a grin. "I'm not trying to be a smart aleck. I just want to draw a distinction here."

Leaning forward again, Davis continued. "My front office doesn't do anything. It's the people who work in my front office who do, say, and think things. Got it?"

Joel nodded. "Good point. Got it."

"So for my front office *team*, it's about them focusing on how they go about their work, and getting them to envision what they sound and look like to the clients."

He slid his chair back slightly and crossed his legs. "Sometimes, if I'm in the right place at the time, I'll listen to them as they take incoming calls. I'll also put myself in a position to hear someone making other calls, like an appointment reminder."

Reaching for his tea cup again, Davis picked it up and finished his point. "I just want to be sure that everyone sounds like they're interested in being here, and that they care about our clients. That's the first and most crucial step in creating client loyalty – having them know that we care."

Joel nodded, attention fixed on Davis's message. Though the noise level in the restaurant remained elevated, neither man seemed to notice as they focused on each other's words.

A server walked nearby, pushing her steam cart, calling out something in Cantonese. Joel looked at Davis with a grin.

"You want anything else while we're waiting for the noodles?"

Davis had been eyeing the cart as soon as it came into view. "Hmm … I really wouldn't mind a little more of the *shiu mai*. Wait – what are those?" He pointed to a small dish containing what looked like three large meatballs.

"Those would be just what they look like … meatballs, Chinese style," replied Joel. He signaled to the server to put the plate on their table. "Try one."

Davis used his chopsticks to stab a meatball and brought it to his plate. After taking a bite, he closed his eyes in appreciation. "These are good," he said, right cheek bulging. "The flavors are incredible!"

Joel watched his lunch companion with amusement. SMILE discussion aside, one of the high points of these meals with Davis was seeing how much the dentist from Long Island enjoyed himself, with all different types of food.

Helping himself to a meatball, Joel returned to the subject at hand. "You were saying that what's key to creating client loyalty is getting them to know that you care."

Davis nodded, still working on his meatball.

"There's a phrase you've probably heard that fits," Joel went on. "It's the one that goes, 'People don't care how much you know, until they know how much you care.' That certainly fits our business, wouldn't you say?"

"Absolutely." Davis had finished the giant meatball and guzzled some more tea. He sat back with a satisfied look on his face.

"But I think a lot of dentists don't have that at the front of their minds," Davis continued. "I think many think they can impress their clients with high-tech equipment, nice looking facilities and such, but leave the chairside manner by the wayside."

"I wouldn't think that would work," said Joel. "Especially if the client is looking for the practice to care about them."

He shifted in his seat and glanced around the busy dining room, eyes drawn for an instant to a toddler with his nose flattened up against one of the mezzanine level turret windows above.

Joel continued, "My problem is trying to get my office staff to care about our clients. The bickering and sniping that can go on, you wouldn't believe. And I'm afraid that attitude might rub off on our clients."

Davis held up a forefinger. "All right, once again, I'm not trying to be a smart aleck. But I think you ought to start thinking about your front office 'staff' as your front office 'team' and have them think of it that way too. Make sense?"

"What's the difference?" Joel spread his hands, palms up.

Davis pursed his lips in thought. "I think, for me, the word 'team' implies a group of individuals working together for the benefit of each other – the team. The word 'staff' feels like a group of people working for one individual."

"Do you think one word makes that much difference?" Joel sounded almost annoyed.

"Why yes, I do," replied Davis. "If they think of themselves as a team, I think it becomes a self-fulfilling prophecy that they eventually act as a team and think of their teammates."

He picked up his tea cup and looked in it before finishing his point. "Besides, what do you have to lose? You yourself said that your team doesn't act like a team, so why not do all you can to encourage being a team?"

"Okay, okay." Joel conceded defeat. "Point taken. I'll promote the team concept and move away from staff."

Davis nodded his approval. "I was about to ask you before, are you able to listen in on your team when they're on the phone? At least to what they're saying and how they say it?"

Joel thought for a moment, his forefinger tracing the rim of his tea cup. "You know, that's probably where I've fallen down. I could, but don't really."

He looked at Davis a bit ruefully. "I guess sometimes I get too ticked off to think of it. Like I don't really know where to start to fix things."

Davis took his turn and refilled Joel's tea cup. "Well, like I said before, you should think of ways to create a culture in your office of showing the client you care. And your front office team needs to buy into it, or you must part company with those who don't."

Leaning forward for emphasis, Davis pressed on. "People in the different job functions of your office team should show that they care in different ways."

Just then he spied the remaining meatball, and looked at Joel with eyebrows raised. "You want that?"

Joel shook his head. "What do you mean, in different ways?"

Davis speared the remaining meatball with his chopsticks. "Your front desk people show they care in the way that they answer the phone, and the way they greet a client when she walks in for an appointment."

He took a bite. Joel waited patiently for Davis to resume talking.

"Your hygienists show they care by the way they greet a client and bring her back to one of the chairs. And they continue to show they care by the way they go about the cleaning and how they explain the treatment the client needs."

Davis drained his tea cup before taking another bite from the meatball. Joel couldn't help but grin again at the obvious display of enjoyment, as he refilled the other man's cup.

Davis went on. "Your dental assistants show they care by how they interact with your clients. For example, depending on who it is, my assistant will reduce the client's anticipational anxiety by explaining the procedure and assuring her that I'm good at making the area numb before starting. After the procedure, she'll tell the client what she can expect once the anesthetic wears off, and go over any other instructions."

"Isn't that pretty typical?" observed Joel.

"Maybe, but I'll bet there are plenty of offices where the assistant doesn't say any of that. Let's take yours, for instance. Do your assistants interact with your clients?" Davis asked Joel.

"Well sort of, but I do most of the talking," admitted Joel.

"So your dental assistants don't really have much dialogue with your clients, other than hello and good-bye?" Davis sounded a little surprised.

"More than just that," replied Joel, a little defensively. "Like I said, I'm the one working on the patient. *Client!*" The other dentist's mouth was half open.

Davis shook his head. "I know that. But you can't be the only one who cares, because you can't be everywhere at once."

Joel looked stumped. "What? What do you mean?"

"Here's what I mean." Davis tossed the remaining portion of meatball into his mouth. Joel could have sworn the man just swallowed that bite whole, like a vitamin pill.

"The client, let's call her Mrs. Miller, knows you care," Davis went on. "But when you leave the room to go to the next client, she's left with your dental assistant. And if your assistant has no dialogue going with Mrs. Miller, after a while Mrs. Miller might think your assistant doesn't care.

"Because you've already gone on to your next client, and Mrs. Miller thinks your assistant doesn't really care about her, she starts thinking your office doesn't really care."

Davis sat back and glared at Joel. "Do you see my point?"

Joel returned the look, uncomfortably silent for the moment. It brought up memories of being questioned in class back in dental school.

He looked up briefly at a nearby chandelier, then said hesitantly, "So, you're saying that even though I create a good relationship with Mrs. Miller, that can be undone if my assistant acts like she doesn't care?"

"Right."

"But Mrs. Miller comes to see me, not my assistant!" protested Joel.

"That's not the point!" Davis threw his hands up in mild exasperation. "The point is making Mrs. Miller feel that *everyone* in your office cares about her!"

He took a chopstick and used it to point at Joel. "*That's* how you start creating customer loyalty!"

With the knuckles of his right hand, Davis reached out and rapped on the table in front of Joel, who was slumped in his chair, staring off into the distance without seeing. "Hello? Are you getting this?" Then Davis broke into a smile.

Frowning, Joel nodded. "I ... think so." His eyes shifted as he met Davis's gaze. "To be honest, I never thought about it this way before. I guess I've been assuming that between me and my dental assistant, I'm the main reason my client is there, so any relationship between my assistant and the client is not really that important."

Brow clearing, Joel sat up and continued. "I've always known about how the front desk and the hygienists can show how they care. I guess I just didn't think it through about how that relates to my dental assistant."

Davis threw his hands up again and exclaimed, "Will you get it through your head, the front desk is a place! Your front desk team are people! Sheesh!" But he grinned widely as the words came out.

Joel cowered in his chair. "Okay! I get it! Don't hurt me." He too had a big grin on his face.

Davis sat back again, nodding in satisfaction. "Well, then, it sounds like I got your attention. So remember, as good a relationship that you, and one or two other people in your office can create with a client, all it takes is one person to change that."

Joel shifted in his seat and reached for his tea cup. "That's certainly true. People remember their bad experiences more than they remember their good ones."

"Doesn't seem fair, does it?" commented Davis. "I once read that a negative story is told thirteen times more often than a positive one." He shrugged. "Go figure. Especially when everyone seems to say that they'll tell everyone they know about your great service."

Joel wore a look of distraction while Davis was talking. "There are certainly plenty of examples where the one bad story is repeated, multiple times."

Joel suddenly sat forward and held up his right hand, palm outward. "I just remembered this story. My sister lives about an hour from Chicago, and before she found the dentist she likes now, she was going to another one someone had told her about. The previous dentist was fine, but what caused my sister to leave that practice was the dental assistant."

He took a drink from his tea cup before continuing. "One day my sister had a problem with tooth #14, so they fit her in for an afternoon appointment. When she got there, and the dental assistant called her in, my sister could see right away that the assistant was mad about something."

Davis listened closely as Joel went on. "The assistant was tossing stuff onto the trays, throwing things into the garbage with extra force, banging the lid, and just making a ruckus in general.

"When my sister asked her 'How are you today?' the assistant didn't even bother answering."

Davis frowned. "What did she – the assistant – say? Anything at all?"

"Nothing. She ignored my sister. It was as if my sister wasn't even in the room."

"How did the visit go when the dentist entered?" asked Davis.

"Just fine," replied Joel. "She always thought the dentist was fine. But by then my sister had enough of the assistant, so when she got home she decided to look for a new dentist. To use her words, she did not want to ever have to lay eyes on that woman again."

Joel finished his tea and studied the bits of tea leaves on the bottom of his cup, as if looking for an answer. "Come to think of it, I guess that's an example of your point earlier, about how a client and the dentist can have a good relationship, but how the assistant can completely undo it."

"Out of curiosity, do you know if your sister has told that story to anyone else other than you?" Davis asked, a slight grin on his face.

"Oh, I'm sure," Joel quickly answered. "She was probably telling the story to her friends when she switched dentists." He stopped. "I get it. There's that 'thirteen times more' thing you mentioned. Well, I don't know that she told thirteen people, but I'm sure she told a bunch."

Davis stroked his jaw. "I just remembered a quote by Warren Buffet, who said 'It takes twenty years to build a reputation and five minutes to ruin it.' Sounds like the assistant took less than five minutes."

He put both hands palms down on the table. "So, does this part all make sense now?"

"It does." Joel nodded emphatically. "I now get the client loyalty piece. Work every day to create loyalty with the client, but beware that it only takes one person to undo the work of everyone else."

He pointed assertively at Davis. "And did you hear? I said it. I used the word 'client'. Twice. How do you like that?" Joel nodded once and sat back, arms folded across his chest.

Just then, a waiter appeared with a large plate of noodles and placed it on their table. Davis's eyes widened at the sight of the fluffy pillow of noodles with its golden brown edges, succulent beef, rich gravy, and crisp vegetables nestled on top. "What do you call this?"

"This is known as beef over crispy noodles, Hong Kong style," said Joel, as he reached for the serving fork and spoon. "Give me your plate, I'll get you started."

Joel expertly handled both serving utensils in one hand, cutting a serving of noodles and toppings in a way that preserved the layered presentation. He deposited the generous portion neatly on Davis's plate.

Davis looked at his plate, then at Joel. "Are there no limits to your talents, Dr. Chenosky?" he exclaimed. "I can only assume your skills handling utensils in the dining room are exceeded only by your handling of instruments in the dental office!" He laughed raucously.

Serving a portion to himself, Joel smiled and started to dig in with his chopsticks. "Let's have a taste of this first, then finish off SMILE with the E."

Summary – "L" = Loyalty

Create client loyalty by showing that you, and everyone in your office, genuinely care about your clients. Be a team, and act as a team!

List the things your office team can do to show they care, and be sure they pay attention to these, each and every day.

• The way they (and you) address and speak to clients, in their phone manner, greetings and good-byes.

• How they (and you) make up for any wrinkles that inconvenience or disappoint the client.

• Their general attitude and demeanor in office.

• Assistants should develop relationships with clients too. This is overlooked by many dentists.

• One person can undo the goodwill created by everyone else.

• Work each and every day to create client loyalty.

Remember what Warren Buffett once said: "It takes twenty years to build a reputation and five minutes to ruin it." This applies to your practice too.

"E" = Equip

*"We must open the doors of opportunity. But we must also equip
our people to walk through those doors."*
--Lyndon B. Johnson

The men enjoyed their crispy noodles for a few moments, not saying much, enveloped by the sights and sounds of the busy New Asia Restaurant dining room. As the lunch hour rush started to wane and people left after finishing their meals, the noise level eased from extreme cacophony to mere chaos.

Joel eyed Davis out of the corner of his eye. The other man certainly knew how to enjoy himself. He thought he could almost hear the sound of Davis's lips smacking, but with all the noise in the dining room, Joel wasn't sure.

He nudged Davis on the arm. "What do you think of the noodles?"

Davis looked up, a couple of noodles hanging from his lower lip. "Awesome," he said, as the delinquent noodle strands quickly disappeared with a sucking sound. He put his chopsticks down to wipe his mouth with his napkin.

"I've never had noodles like these before," he said. "Whenever I have this back at home, it's takeout Chinese, and those noodles don't taste at all like these."

"These are the real thing, that's for sure," agreed Joel, picking the last few bits off his plate. "Want some more? There's plenty left."

"Still working on this." Davis picked up his chopsticks again.

"All right Professor, I can't believe we've reached the E in SMILE." Joel exaggerated a smile by showing his teeth for effect, which went unnoticed by the other dentist because he was focused on his plate again.

"I know from your reference card that the E stands for Equip, but I'm going to guess that means that you must have the right equipment in the office to wow your clients and build loyalty."

Davis, jaw still in perpetual motion, shook his head. "Again, right word, wrong application." He shoved another load of noodles into his mouth.

Joel refilled both their tea cups from the teapot, and waited patiently until Davis could continue.

Davis put his chopsticks down, sat back and swallowed his latest mouthful. Picking up his tea cup, he took a swig from it, then finished his thought.

"The Equip in SMILE has to do with equipping your people with the right tools – actually that's partly related to equipment – but more importantly the right knowledge to use the tools effectively."

"You mean getting the training from the system vendors and all that," Joel stated.

Davis took another pull from his cup. "That's only part of it. You have to be sure that your team internalizes the knowledge too, and uses whatever systems they have to the best of their benefit."

"Now you're sounding like an equipment rep," complained Joel.

"No, I mean it," persisted Davis. "Too many people go to training, then they come back and they don't use the system or piece of equipment any differently than they did before they went.

"Or, the onsite trainer arrives, gives the lunchtime learning session, leaves, and everyone still uses the system in the same way."

Joel nodded in agreement. "I have to admit, we've had some of that happen in my office."

Davis picked up his chopsticks again and held out his plate. "Uh, can I get a little more of that?"

While Joel served up another portion, Davis continued. "It doesn't matter what type of equipment we're talking about, whether it's hardware like CEREC, The Wand, GALILEOS, or even practice management software like SoftDent or EagleSoft. Training alone doesn't necessarily turn your team into power users. Internalizing the training is what equips them."

Joel returned Davis's plate to him, now loaded up again. "Thanks Joel."

"So how do you internalize it, as you say?" asked Joel, taking a sip from his tea cup.

Davis had resumed the eating position. "You work it in to your meetings."

Joel leaned forward to catch that. "In to my meetings? You mean we do the training as part of one of my meetings?"

"No." Davis shook his head, not missing a beat with his noodles. "I mean after your team gets trained on something, you work the discussion of that training into your regular meetings. That might be you asking how they're doing with the new system or piece of equipment. It might be you asking them to show the group certain things on the system so you know that they know."

He paused to drink some tea from his cup.

"It's like testing them on their post-training knowledge, so to speak?" asked Joel.

"Partly that. But it's mainly to keep the dialogue going so the knowledge can stay fresh in your team members' minds." Davis grinned, looking down at his plate, almost empty again. "Boy, this is really good."

"One of the frustrations I have is that one person in my office might be the expert on my Dexis system, for example," observed Joel. "Then everyone else goes to that person for questions, and it's lost productivity everywhere."

Davis pointed his chopsticks at Joel again and nodded. "Exactly. And that's why cross-training is important, too. What if you have someone who's out for a little while? Or, let's say your front desk person is unavailable, and the hygienist answers the phone? She should know how to look up a client's info or appointment schedule."

Joel responded, "They do know. I think. Well, maybe I'm not so sure."

Davis cleaned the rest of his plate and lined his chopsticks up neatly on it. "And don't forget, it's not just about training on how to use the equipment or system, it's also how you assign responsibility for maintenance and supplies."

He pointed at Joel. "For example, do you have someone responsible for calling support if one of your pieces of equipment needs attention? Or do you do it?"

"I do it, if they're not sure about it," Joel confessed.

"Well, you can't have them be 'not sure' about it," Davis admonished. "Let's say they were to know way more about your CEREC than you do. They'd probably make the call on their own. You've got to equip them so they have the level of knowledge that allows them to do that."

Joel protested, "But they don't seem interested in it. That's my beef with them right now, not taking responsibility!" His closed fist pounded the table as frustration welled quickly again.

"That may have been the case before, but you didn't have the S in SMILE. And you're now working on your clear and simple objectives," Davis reminded him. "When you're done, you'll be better able to see who's all in, and who's not. Right?"

"Right." Joel nodded weakly. The mood swings could get tiring sometimes. He looked at his hand and thought he could still see a slight bruise from when he pounded the stone fountain in Ghirardelli Square the first morning.

Davis sat back, folded his napkin, and laid it on the table. "This is just part of the broader picture of the E, being able to equip your team to do their jobs. It's not just the vendor training, it's not just internalizing the knowledge, it's not just maintenance and supplies."

He thought for a moment, fingers steepled as he pondered an overhead chandelier. His gaze dropped to meet Joel's again.

"You know what it is, it's you being able to create a process for your people, on how you deal with outside vendors and their equipment or systems that you use in your practice. That includes how you internally use the systems or equipment."

Joel looked a little lost, but waited for Davis to clarify.

"See how this works?" Davis started to rev up. "I never really thought about it this way, I guess because I've never had to talk about it in depth like I've been talking with you."

He rubbed his palms together and leaned forward, elbows resting on his knees.

"Let's just use EagleSoft as an example, and let's say you convert to EagleSoft. You get trained by them, and your team has the overview knowledge from that training. Then your people start using the system, and run into the usual questions and problems early on that anyone can have with an unfamiliar system.

"Who do they ask? Each other? Or maybe they call support. In that case, which one calls support? And when that person gets the answer, does that person share the answer with everyone else, or does she just go back to doing what she was doing?"

Davis sat up straight, energized by his narrative. "You're the guy who must put the process in place for this. You determine, okay, if anybody has a question, first ask Sally or Marge. Then if they don't know, either Sally or Marge calls support. After she gets the answer, the next office meeting, she's responsible for sharing the result. And so on."

Joel saw his point. "So you're saying it's the process itself that helps equip the staff – uh, the team?"

"Yes." Davis drew his hands apart in the air like he was painting a picture. "The process helps people figure out what they do in certain situations, and also doles out the responsibilities for different pieces of equipment or systems in the office."

Davis stabbed his finger emphatically in Joel's direction. "So you don't have to do it yourself all the time. Or so your people don't get you to do what they should be doing."

Just then, Davis froze at the sight of the plate of *don tut* still sitting on the table. "Hey, we forgot to eat those!"

He reached for one, taking the flaky pastry tart out of its paper shell. After taking a bite comprising almost half of the delicacy, he closed his eyes and shook his head.

"Wow, this is amazing," he gushed.

Joel grinned at the sight of the other dentist, yet again enjoying himself to the max. What was more amazing was that Davis had overlooked the plate of treats until now. "Good, huh?"

Davis nodded, mouth full. He had popped the other half in there, and sat licking his fingers.

"Back to this process you're talking about, how would I lay this all out, so they know who's responsible for what?" asked Joel. He reached for a *don tut*, figuring he'd better claim one before they all disappeared.

"Remember when I talked about job descriptions, when we talked about the M in SMILE?" Davis wiped some egg custard from his chin. "That's where you can put that in."

Joel rubbed the side of his jaw. "I don't have any of that in place right now. I'd be practically starting from scratch," he whined.

"That's the beauty of it, my friend!" cried Davis. "It's almost like you can start with a clean slate."

"Yes, but I've got the people I've got," observed Joel glumly.

"That might actually make it a little easier," Davis said. "You know the folks you have, you know what their strengths and weaknesses are. Well, I assume you do."

Joel concurred with a nod. "I do at that. Like I said, there seem to be more weaknesses than strengths right now."

"But you and I agreed that this is a chicken-and-egg situation, since you don't have a simple set of objectives, and job descriptions for your team." Davis didn't want to let Joel off the hook. "After you put those in place, you'll be better able to manage and guide your people to get them to do the right things."

Joel shrugged. "Can't disagree with you there, I guess."

The two men fell silent and for the next moment, looked around the dining room that by now was only half full. Joel turned back to Davis.

"Have you found that any particular job category is more suited to certain tasks? Like I should assign certain pieces of equipment to a particular person because of what they do?"

Davis thought for a moment before answering. "There are some things that are probably more natural fits. In my office, my dental assistants perform maintenance on the sterilization equipment. They're also in charge of the software updates to the scanners and CEREC. My admin team is responsible for any computer upgrades, and updates to the billing software."

"They're responsible for all those technical details?" asked Joel, sounding almost doubtful.

"Sure." Davis shrugged. "They can handle it. Besides, don't forget that knowing this can lead to a sense of accomplishment on their part, from being the office expert at something."

He paused again to think, as he tapped his fingertips lightly on the tablecloth covering the table. "For the other things, I tend to match them up by who works the most with what. Everyone has to be somewhat technically inclined anyway, because they're using the practice management software and other technology at different times throughout the day.

"So for example, my dental assistants need to do any online reordering of disposables and preventives. My admin team makes sure we have the office supplies and breakroom or janitorial items we need, and reorders those when necessary."

Joel nodded absent-mindedly, and Davis continued.

"Whoever reorders disposables or supplies needs to be conscious of the overall budget, and trade that off with bulk savings opportunities," said Davis. "It might be cheaper per piece to buy in larger quantities, but I never want to be supply-rich and cash-poor."

Joel had been half-listening because his thoughts started to wander again. "Well, I guess what I need to do is continue what I started the other night in my room, and lay it all out. Figure out my simple objectives, and figure out who on my office team does what."

"Right, then communicate it, remind them of it, and hold them to it." Davis made a gesture suggestive of tying a knot.

"Besides," he continued, "you never know. Your people could have been waiting for more structure and guidance all this time. They might embrace new responsibilities and feel new energy from being challenged."

Joel pursed his lips with a slight frown. "Well, I hope so." He was quiet for a moment, then asked, "You've found your SMILE system works for you?"

"No question," said Davis without hesitation. "Remember what I told you the first day we met, that we had a good year not because we had a lot of new clients, but more because we were better-connected with our existing ones?"

Joel nodded. "That was what you said that caught my attention. Other than the 'clients' versus 'patients' thing." He grinned.

"Right, so every part of SMILE allowed us to better connect with our clients," Davis replied. "Obviously, the S, M, and the I help you focus on building the right team of people and getting them to do the right things. The L is focused on creating client loyalty."

"But what about the E?" Joel pointed out. "Having a good process in itself doesn't necessarily translate to connecting with clients."

"*Au contraire*, my friend," countered Davis. He raised his hand. "When you have a strong E, your people know what they should be doing to use all your technology and equipment in the most efficient way. Errors are at a minimum, everyone looks like they know what they're doing, and your office seems to hum along smoothly."

He stood up. "That feeling of a finely tuned machine, so to speak, along with the clients knowing that we care, definitely helps us better connect with them."

Davis looked around. "Excuse me for a moment. I feel like I drank a gallon of tea." He headed off in the direction of the rest rooms.

Left alone at the table, Joel recounted what Davis had said. It makes sense, he thought, and it all seemed to be falling in place, as far as what he should be thinking about and doing.

In his pocket, Joel's cell phone vibrated. Even though the bedlam of the dining room had subsided, there was no way he could hear the ringer. He reached for the device and saw that it was Lora.

"Hello honey, how are you?"

"Am I interrupting anything?" Back in Denver, Lora was in the car headed back to their house.

"No, Davis and I are just about done here. When he gets back from the men's room I'll probably take care of the check and head out."

"Are you all set with checking out of the hotel?" Lora took the access ramp to the freeway.

"Did it before we left for lunch. And I've still got plenty of time to get to SFO for my flight."

"So how was the trip overall, dear?"

Joel leaned forward to put his elbows on the table. "It was good, and all because I happened to meet Davis.

Actually, I'm kind of excited. Now I have an idea of what I have to figure out to maybe, just maybe, help get our office back on track."

"Really!" Lora was surprised, but glad to hear the new level of energy in her husband's voice. "Well, I want to hear all about it when you get home tonight."

"You will." Joel looked up as Davis returned to the table. "I'll call you again just before I get ready to board." They said their goodbyes and Joel ended the call.

With a grin, Joel said to Davis as he sat down, "All set? Want anything more to eat?"

Davis put his hand on his stomach. "Oh, no, I don't think I can put anything else in here." He looked around and lowered his voice. "That is, until dinner!" He laughed.

Over Davis's objections, Joel paid for lunch. The two men left the cavernous dining room through the front entrance's narrow keyhole walkway, and emerged onto the sunlit sidewalk outside.

"How are you doing on time, since you have to meet your wife?" asked Joel, as he checked his watch.

"I'm good," replied Davis. "But what about you? You have a flight to catch."

"I've got plenty of time. Let's catch a cab back to the Wharf so I can rescue my bags and head out."

The return trip seemed to take only half the time it took them to get to the restaurant. Their taxi headed straight up Pacific, made a right on Stockton, and took that all the way to Beach Street. A left turn, and minutes later, the two men stood by the front entrance of Joel's hotel.

Joel turned to Davis. "Well, this is it, man. I take leave of you here." He smiled warmly and extended his hand. "Thanks so much for spending all the time with me these past few days, and even more so for giving me the benefit of your wisdom, your SMILE system, and your perspective."

Davis took Joel's hand and grasped it firmly. "It was my pleasure, my friend. Actually, talking about SMILE helped me too. It's always good to do a sanity check once in a while to be sure what I'm doing makes sense to someone else."

"If you don't mind, I'll stay in touch and let you know how it goes over the next few months," said Joel. "I've got a lot of thinking to do, a lot of things to figure out, a lot of new ground to cover, but I'll tell you – for the first time in a long time, I'm excited."

Davis smiled broadly. "That's terrific. Of course I want to hear what happens. Oh, and by the way, many thanks again for being my culinary guide to San Francisco!" He patted his stomach. "I've never eaten so well in my life, and I think I gained fifteen pounds eating out with you!"

Both men laughed, and with a final wave, parted ways. Joel went in to get his bags, as Davis continued on toward his hotel.

Summary – "E" = Equip

Just having the equipment or systems doesn't empower your office team to deliver their best. Equipping your team with the knowledge of using it effectively and efficiently is what can make your practice shine.

• Strive to internalize any vendor training for staying power.

• Cross-train team members so they can cover for others when necessary.

• Create a process to internalize training (e.g. via meetings), and also support calls and results, and who maintains which systems (including supplies).

• This process must be in place, with everyone understanding it and knowing their roles.

• Include related process responsibilities in each team member's job description.

• Utilize the regular meetings to troubleshoot, reinforce, re-train, or re-educate as necessary.

The key to a strong E in SMILE is to have a process with assigned responsibilities, and for everyone to buy in and be accountable.

Epilogue

"I can't change the direction of the wind, but I can adjust my sails to always reach my destination."

--Jimmy Dean

Mid-May in the Denver region is always a beautiful time. With flowers and trees well in bloom, mountains still snow-capped and not yet tinged by smog, it almost feels like the arrival of summer is just around the corner.

Inside his office, Joel looked at his watch, calculating the time difference between the Mountain and Eastern time zones. Davis ought to be at lunch about now, he thought, as he picked up the phone and punched in the numbers.

"Hello, thank you for calling the offices of Dr. Avalon," said the voice from Long Island.

"Hello," Joel responded, "I was calling for Dr. Avalon. Would he be available to take a quick call during his lunch hour?"

"Well, I'll be happy to ask. Who's calling please?"

"It's Dr. Joel Chenosky."

"Can you hold for a moment? I'll be right back."

"Thank you."

After a few seconds, Joel heard a click as the line was picked up.

"Joel! … Davis here. What a pleasant surprise! How are you, my friend?"

"Great, Davis. I hope I'm not interrupting your lunch," said Joel. He broke into a grin at the sound of the other man's voice.

"Nah, nothing special for lunch anyway. Actually, lunches are rarely special any more, after you spoiled me with all those great meals in San Francisco last fall!" He laughed heartily into the phone before continuing.

"And by the way, thank you again for the Boudin sourdough at Christmas! What a treat, man, I was so excited. Even my wife said to me, how can anyone get so excited about bread?"

Joel smiled at the memory of having had the exact same thought back in San Francisco. "I'm glad you enjoyed it."

"So what's up? Are you calling me to tell me that you're coming to Long Island soon? If you are, it'll be my turn to take you on a culinary tour."

"I'm afraid I don't have any travel plans yet, but I was calling you to tell you about how SMILE has worked out for me." Joel leaned back in his chair and put his feet up on his desk.

1,800 miles away in his Long Island office, Davis swiveled his desk chair and sat down. "Fire away. In fact, just the other day I was wondering how you were doing with it."

"Well, it was interesting," Joel began. "When I first returned home from San Francisco, I continued to think through the things you got me started on when you took me through your SMILE process."

He stood up, turned, and perched on the edge of his desk. "I set up my simple-to-communicate objectives, figured out my regular meeting schedule and agendas, decided who should be doing what, and created job descriptions."

Davis listened intently. "How did your people react to all of that?"

"At first, they weren't sure what I was up to," confessed Joel. "But I explained to them that we had to figure out how to do things differently, or all of us wouldn't be doing anything at all. That seemed to catch their attention."

"I'll bet that was the first time you expressed that type of thought to them," Davis ventured.

"It was," admitted Joel. "I guess I'd been hiding my fears from them prior to going to San Francisco."

He stood and started pacing in front of his desk. "And once I did, surprisingly enough, they seemed interested in trying to help out. I guess they didn't necessarily want to lose their jobs either."

"It's not just that," Davis observed. "It's also a show of trust when you share with them the issues you're trying to solve, and give them the opportunity to help you solve them."

"Definitely." Joel stopped his pacing and stared straight at his computer monitor, not seeing what was on it. He went on to quickly summarize for Davis what transpired over the next several months.

"Sounds like they accepted the challenge and started to take some ownership for what they should be doing," said Davis after Joel finished talking.

"They did," agreed Joel. "Mind you, there's still work to be done – it's still a work in progress. Not only for them, but for me too. I've had to change the way I look at things over the past few months."

"Did you have to part ways with anyone?" Davis pivoted his chair in short left and right movements as he spoke.

"Not so far," answered Joel. "I was most worried about my office manager, but after a little bit of a bumpy start, she seems to have settled in to the new normal of things."

Joel sat down in his chair again, and resumed the position with his feet up on his desk. "Of the entire office team, she seemed the most offended when I presented her with her job description."

"Was that because her duties changed drastically?"

"No, her duties didn't really change all that much," said Joel. "At least, not from what I'd been thinking she should be doing all along. I think she was just miffed about the idea of being held accountable to a list of duties on paper."

"Sounds like you're on the right track, Joel." Davis looked up as one of his dental assistants motioned to him from the hallway. He nodded and held up his hand, three fingers extended.

"Like I said, it's still a work in progress, but I do feel pretty good about it right now," said Joel. "In fact, it looks like this quarter we're going to see our first quarter-over-quarter revenue increase in a long while!"

"That's terrific! Congratulations Joel!"

"Thanks, Davis. Look, I'd better let you get going." Joel glanced at his watch. "I know you have to get back to work, but I wanted to give you an update. I also wanted to tell you again that I couldn't be doing this without your help. And all the time you generously gave me back in San Francisco."

Davis smiled into his phone. "Well, my friend, I'm glad things are looking up for you. The pleasure was all mine. And my stomach's pleasure too!" He laughed so loudly that a couple of his office team members looked in to see what was going on.

Joel laughed. "Many thanks again, Davis. All the best to you and your family."

"Right back at you, Joel. And remember, if you make it to Long Island, you'd better be calling me first!"

"I will. Take care."

With that, the dentists ended their phone call. Joel put the phone back in its cradle on his desk. For a long moment he sat, elbows on his knees, contemplating the phone, a smile reflecting his thoughts.

Susan, his office manager, stepped into Joel's office. "Do you have a minute? It's about that report you wanted me to run, showing clients without appointments who haven't been in for longer than six months, then cross-checking it against the different insurance plans?"

Joel turned to face her. "What about it?"

"Well, I figured out how to do it! I'm so excited I can't wait to show you!" She ran out of the room.

Joel sat for a moment longer, shook his head, and chuckled to himself. He rose from his chair and walked down the hallway, following her.

SMILE for Higher Profits!

S is for **Simple**

M is for **Manage**

I is for **Initiative**

L is for **Loyalty**

E is for **Equip**

Simple. Create strategic objectives for your practice that are simple to understand, simple to communicate, and simple to remember. These will create a "guiding light" for your team's daily behaviors and decision-making.

Manage. Manage to your objectives. Hold your team members accountable to achieving your practice's overall objectives.

Initiative. Surround yourself with people who have initiative. Do not tolerate anyone who takes action only when you tell them to.

Loyalty. Work each and every day to create and build client loyalty, by showing how much you care. All of your office team members' behaviors should align with this.

Equip. Equip your team with the knowledge and processes that will allow them to excel at what they do, making all of you look good.

About Gary Lim, M.A.

Gary Lim, M.A., is a consultant, senior business advisor, and president of Aurarius LLC, a management consulting firm he first founded in California's Silicon Valley then relocated to Upstate New York. He is also co-founder of HealthcareBusinessOffice LLC, and his past business experience includes leadership positions at larger firms such as Hewlett-Packard, ROLM, XEROX, and Novell, and at small companies and start-ups.

A seasoned and energetic public speaker, Gary has spoken to audiences in many venues, including keynote addresses, conference workshops, corporate/executive seminars, product launches, and training courses. He has worked with thousands of attendees from organizations ranging from Fortune 500 corporations and mid-market firms to not-for-profits and educational institutions.

As an author, *SMILE!* is Gary's fifth released work. His first, *The Road to Gumption: Using Your Inner Courage to Balance Your Work and Personal Life* (Dorato Press) was an Amazon #1 Bestseller in its category. Next came *Let It Fly! Defy the Laws of Business Gravity and Keep Your Company Soaring*, a business parable featuring effective business leadership principles and a story set at a well-known golf course along the Pacific Ocean. Then came the original *Dive Into ACTION! Find Your Niche in Times of Uncertainty*, and *Dive Into ACTION! for Recent Graduates*, both books on the topic of finding new career opportunities.

In his work with business owners, executives, client organizations, seminar attendees, and at company meetings, Gary brings to bear his ability to assess a complex business situation, identify the critical issues, and offer practical insights for solutions.

He earned a Bachelor's degree *cum laude* in Electrical Engineering and Computer Science from Princeton University, and a Master's degree in Organizational Management from University of Phoenix. For over ten years, Gary held the appointment of Visiting Professor of Entrepreneurship at SUNY College of Environmental Science and Forestry in Syracuse, New York.

To inquire about speaking engagements, custom seminars, and advisory services, reach out to Gary directly:

Blog/Website: http://myActionPronto.com
Book information: www.SmileToElevate.com
Email contact: Gary@SmileToElevate.com
Phone contact: 315-885-1532

About Bruce Stewart, D.D.S.

Dr. Bruce Stewart earned his D.D.S. at the University of Buffalo School of Dentistry. After serving his residency at Upstate Medical Center in Syracuse, then a four-year associateship, Dr. Stewart began his practice in Oneida, New York in 1987. His focus is on bringing technology to the practice to elevate his clients' dental experience.

Notes

www.ingramcontent.com/pod-product-compliance
Lightning Source LLC
Chambersburg PA
CBHW060035210326
41520CB00009B/1133